DEBATING
SOUTHERN
HISTORY

Debating Twentieth-Century America

Series Editor: James T. Patterson, Brown University

DEBATING SOUTHERN HISTORY

Ideas and Action
in the Twentieth Century

BRUCE CLAYTON
and
JOHN SALMOND

ROWMAN & LITTLEFIELD PUBLISHERS, INC.
Lanham • Boulder • New York • Oxford

ROWMAN & LITTLEFIELD PUBLISHERS, INC.

Published in the United States of America
by Rowman & Littlefield Publishers, Inc.
4720 Boston Way, Lanham, Maryland 20706
http://www.rowmanlittlefield.com

12 Hid's Copse Road
Cumnor Hill, Oxford OX2 9JJ, England

British Library Cataloguing in Publication Information Available

Library of Congress Cataloging-in-Publication Data
Clayton, Bruce.
    Debating southern history : ideas and action in the twentieth
century / Bruce Clayton and John Salmond.
        p.   cm.—(Debating twentieth-century America)
    Includes bibliographical references and index.
    ISBN 0-8476-9413-5 (cloth: alk. paper).—ISBN 0-8476-9414-3
(pbk. : alk. paper)
    1. Southern States—History—1865–1951 Sources.   2. Southern
States—History—1951– Sources.   3. Southern States—History—
1865–1951—Historiography.   I. Salmond, John A.   II. Title.
III. Series.
F215.C66   1999
975'.04—dc21   99-37014
                                                                          CIP

Printed in the United States of America

CONTENTS

FOREWORD

Debating Twentieth-Century America is a series of books aimed at helping readers appreciate an important aspect of the writing of history: there is no simple, wholly agreed-on "truth" that captures what has happened in the past. Our understanding of the events of history depends considerably on the way that individual historians interpret them.

With this in mind, each book in the series features two essays, written from varying perspectives, about an important issue, event, or trend in twentieth-century American history. The essayists, who are well-known writers and teachers in their fields, bring to this task considerable expertise. They have delved into the primary and secondary sources and have arrived at personal interpretations of their subjects. Their conclusions, however, reflect different approaches or conclusions. Placed side by side, as in this book, the essays frequently engage in "debate" over the past.

The sources for the essays in this book are far too numerous and varied to reprint in full here. Still, the writers of the essays in *Debating Twentieth-Century America* wish to give readers a sense of the evidence for their generalizations. They therefore include a small number of documents that have influenced their thinking. Readers may find it challenging to evaluate the relevance and importance of these documents.

We hope that the essays and documents will help readers understand the complexity of the past, as well as the subjective process of writing history that carries the past to the present.

James T. Patterson

INTRODUCTION

These two essays have been concerned with ideas and action, and with the complex relationship between them. The connection is most obvious in our treatment of the civil rights revolution, and the overshadowing influence of Dr. Martin Luther King, Jr., surely the most significant Southerner of the past fifty years. Mr. Clayton's essay traces in detail the evolution of Dr. King's thought, how his understanding of the scriptures, his exploration of Gandhi's philosophy of non-violent resistance, the notions of human purpose that he learned from such theologians as Reinhold Niebuhr and Walter Rauschenbusch, eventually came together in a specific revolutionary ideology. Mr. Salmond's essay describes how these ideas were translated into political action, and how they influenced thousands of young people, black and white, into eventually challenging the southern caste system in what became America's most significant social revolution. Martin King is the most important linking figure in the years covered by these essays.

There are, of course, many other examples of such links. Mr. Clayton discusses the strains of southern thought, in the years before World War II, which eventually led to a thorough-going critique of the region's economic backwater, its social institutions, its folk-ways. He shows, in particular, how influential Howard Odum was in fashioning this critique and how much of the 1938 report on the Economic Conditions of the South was influenced by this work. This report, too, became action, became part of the stuff of American politics in 1938, as Mr. Salmond's essay shows.

1

More broadly, the report provided the impetus for the foundation of the Southern Conference for Human Welfare, and a blueprint for political and social advocacy throughout the succeeding decade.

Mr. Clayton's essay, too, shows that there were always white Southerners whose thinking led them to challenge accepted southern traditions, not only in politics or in race relations, but also in their personal lives. He has used Lillian Smith as his prime example of the southern liberal intellectual, writing from outside safe boundaries. Mr. Salmond shows how Smith's thought led her to embrace the civil rights movement, when it came, to join forces, in effect, with Martin Luther King.

Thus, these two essays form a whole. Together, they tell the story of southern change, from the philosophers, writers, and historians of the 1920s who first challenged the social conformity and economic backwardness of their region, through those few brave souls who in the New Deal years attempted to translate these notions into political solutions, till, in the years after the second world war, ideas and action came together to forge a powerful instrument of transformation.

Bruce Clayton and John Salmond

SOUTHERN INTELLECTUALS

Bruce Clayton

A t the heart of this book's two essays stands a question: who speaks for the South? Until recently, the historian's answer was clear. White men, from Thomas Jefferson to William Faulkner to Jimmy Carter, would have been the obvious, perhaps unconscious answer—white men speak for "the South." This book argues that by the end of World War I in 1918, a debate had begun: who or what is the South, and who speaks for it? At first, in the 1920s, one would have needed a very sensitive ear to have heard the voices of the long submerged "other" South—blacks, male and female, and white women. By the 1930s and early 1940s these voices—often moderate and well-mannered, but sometimes angry, even shrill—were being heard. Few Southerners of either race or gender even guessed that, in what might appear to have been an undirected, unfocused babble of words and actions, the way was being prepared for the most historic event of the twentieth-century South, the Civil Rights Movement. By concentrating first on intellectuals—people who make it their business to think, and to think as critically as possible—and then social activists from 1920 to 1965, this book follows the twists and turns and the many bumpy roads that Southerners, in all their diversity, had to travel to get to the place and time when "the South" meant everybody who calls the region home. No one would argue that the South is perfect. And no region or country has a monopoly on goodness—or evil. While accepted by the majority, the great

3

change in the South is still being slandered and resisted (again, sometimes violently) by some Southerners.

Given that diversity and these changes, does it make sense to identify anything as "southern"? It does, if only because all Southerners before 1965 assumed or spoke of various things as specific to their region. The South—defined here as the eleven Confederate states plus Kentucky and Oklahoma—may exist only in the mind, and there are many Souths. Hence today one is foolish to speak of "the mind of the South." And yet, as the esteemed C. Vann Woodward said in his "Search for Southern Identity," Southerners are Americans, but they know and feel some special things in common. The rest of the country has been far more affluent. The South has suffered "generations of scarcity." In many pockets of the South that is still true. Yankees (before Vietnam) were successful, won major world wars, and thought themselves invincible, entitled to wear the red badge of courage. The South lost the Civil War and has lived with that memory. The North, in applying the nation's cherished beliefs to itself, was born in innocence and devoted to freedom. But the South? It had slavery, the nation's "great evil," and then legalized racial segregation, known as Jim Crow. And last, according to Woodward, Northerners are abstract; as "Americans" they live, if only in their confident identity, anywhere and everywhere in the nation. Not Southerners. They are concrete; they do not live "everywhere," they live in Richmond, Virginia, or Oxford, Mississippi, or Charleston, South Carolina, or Little Rock, Arkansas. Southerners have a sense of place, a specific place that in its largest sense is "the South" and *then* America.[1]

To Woodward's list of what it means to be (or feel) southern this book adds that Southerners have had a deep sense of race, perhaps an obsession with color. They have also had, if statistics mean anything, a consuming commitment to religion—not to some generalized allegiance to faith, but to a specific church. Certainly down to 1965 (and very likely even today) Southerners have had a deep, enduring sense of family, of the value and fun of sports, of leisure, of music, particularly music that flows from a folk culture. Is it surprising that the Grand Ol' Opry is in Nashville, Tennessee, that Memphis welcomes everybody to visit Graceland, where Elvis Presley lived, and that Tupelo, Mississippi, wants the world to know that the King of rock and roll was born there?

Country music is southern. And the blues, if they did not originate in the Mississippi Delta region, matured there, just as traditional jazz was born down river on the Mississippi in New Orleans, and western swing took wings in Texas. The banjo, an African survival among slaves, is to Southerners what the violin (as opposed to its country-fried namesake, the fiddle) is to Northerners. Add one last thing in this treacherous effort to identify certain traits as unique to a region: Southerners, being folks who aren't very abstract, have had a great tradition of telling stories—whether it is a honky tonk song by Patsy Cline or Hank Williams or a tale told by Tennessee Williams or Zora Neale Hurston. Stories, often the staple of southern sermons, are often embellished and carried along on the wings of rhetoric, sometimes rhetorical excess, which is perhaps another part of southern identity.

The South has no monopoly on these traits; nor would Southerners want to be identified with all of them, anymore than they would want to be thought of as people who would die if deprived of pork barbecue, fried chicken, catfish, collard greens, black-eyed peas, or sweet iced tea—or a big black diamond watermelon from the Piggly Wiggly grocery chain started by a Southerner. Trying to say what makes something "southern" is likely to get one court martialed by academics. But having walked the plank this far, the authors contend that only a non-Southerner would be surprised to learn that Bessie Smith defines the blues or that William Faulkner's *The Sound and the Fury* or Margaret Mitchell's *Gone With the Wind* could have been written only by someone who was born and bred in the South.

THE SOUTHERN INTELLECTUAL SCENE: 1920S

In 1920, the South looked bleak and forbidding to many young Southerners of intellectual or literary aspirations. This was especially true for anyone with an independent streak, anyone with an inkling of the cultural world beyond Dixie. The South had not one first-class university and few readers of serious books. Dixie boasted no symphony orchestra of any standing—and no major library, publishing house, newspaper, or magazine remotely comparable to those in the North. There were a few writers of distinction, novelists such as the Virginians, Ellen Glasgow and James Branch Cabell, but the region's most popular writers of the pre-1914 generation had written now-forgotten racist novels or highly sentimental fiction that glorified the Old South.

"Down there," scoffed the social critic H. L. Mencken in 1917, "a poet is now almost as rare as an oboe-player . . . or a metaphysician." Mencken was a caustic, nationally known, cigar-chomping Baltimore journalist who liked to consider himself something of a southern gentleman, given his Maryland birth. But he labeled the South "The Sahara of the Bozart," a vast intellectual wasteland. Any creative endeavor, from architecture to theology, Mencken observed as "an awe-inspiring blank."[2]

Mencken's criticisms were usually exaggerated and unfair, and Southerners by the score despised him. But most importantly, his attacks established the central issues southern writers and intellectuals would address for the next decades. At the heart of Mencken's censures was the question: what is the artist or intellectual's relationship to the prevailing culture? The issue was acute by the 1920s, particularly for younger Southerners—most of them born around 1900—who shared in the national mood of rebellion against traditional ways of thinking and behavior. The modernist era of the flapper, Freudianism, bootleg gin, and jazz had begun.

For many Southerners in the 1920s their revolt would be against the sentimentalists and the apostles of a New South, the post-Civil War generations coming of age in the 1880s and 1890s. The apostles of the New South were men like Henry W. Grady of the *Atlanta Constitution* and Walter Hines Page, a North Carolinian who became a major literary figure from his editorial base in New York City. Grady coined the expression, "New South," and Page published and spoke for a host of self-styled progressive thinkers of the pre-1914 era. They were, with a few exceptions, white, male, middle-class professionals who devoutly believed that the South should be made over in the image of the bustling North. The engines of change would be cosmopolitan new cities, factories, public schools, and the newly established Jim Crow laws that legalized racial segregation. The new racial laws were "reforms," said politicians, professors, and preachers, many of whom, like the Reverend Edgar Gardner Murphy, were genuine reformers in their fight against child labor and their battles for public education. Intellectuals such as Walter Hines Page argued that segregation, by separating the races "fairly," would curtail racial friction and the excessive anger of the white masses. Such was the creed of progress, sometimes called New South Liberalism, which flowered one last time in 1925 in Edward Mims's appropriately titled book, *The Advancing South*.

But to many coming of age in the 1920s—such as Faulkner, or the social critic Lillian Smith, or African-American writers like Zora Neale Hurston and Richard Wright—Mims's optimism was well-meaning but out of date, "Victorian," some said. New ideas were needed, contended writers of all shades of opinion—from the precocious Allen Tate, avant-garde in his poetry but conservative in his social views, to historians as diverse as W. J. Cash and Woodward. For them, a truly advancing South needed to look critically at every moment of its past, examine itself carefully, and seek solutions far beyond humming textile mills and paternalistic race relations.

In introducing intellectuals, much will be made of modernism to explain the ways in which Southerners were coming to think about themselves and their region. Modernism's roots are in the nineteenth century, but it flowered in the twentieth. In art it meant experimenting with new images, whether cubes or ordinary soup cans; in music modernists sought not lovely sounds but whatever notes, however discordant, were needed to represent the world they had inherited. Poets sought the inner voice of feeling, whether or not the words rhymed. Experimentation, originality, creativity—these, and not rules or traditions from the past, were the assumptions of modernists.

Modernist intellectuals assumed a belief in the psychological centrality not of rational thought but of human emotions; of irrationality both in individuals and society; of the importance of class, race, biology (and sex, now called gender) in determining how we think and act. Modernists assume that irony, paradox, and ambiguity are inherent in any social situation—just as personal passions are inherent in individuals. During the nineteenth century, "Victorians" knew that people and society were amenable to control by rational exhortations to be moral and ethical—and that evil resulted from ignorance or the lack of rational leadership. Rationality, by giving us a clear picture of ourselves and the world, keeps us from becoming animals or savages. Modernists would love to believe that, but they have to argue that the best we can do is to make some sort of contact with an ever changing, usually unpredictable, reality. Victorians assumed a duality between humans and the material world, between reason and emotions, with rationality enabling us to control ourselves and our world. That duality, however comforting, is denied to modernists, who think that individuals are intricately involved in the very world they would measure and control. "Whirl is king," said Carl L. Becker, a perceptive historian of ideas. In summing up modernism, Becker stressed that the duty of a thinker is to accept change and to try to think critically about what "whirl" might bring if left unchecked. No one studied in these pages would subscribe to all of the above principles. But virtually all were some shade of modernist.[3]

The South in 1920 was a backward, rural folk culture honeycombed with lynchings, race riots, and Jim Crow laws. To make things worse, most Southerners viewed critical thinking and ideas, except religious creeds, with suspicion, often contempt. Of course, not everyone of intellectual or artistic temperament agreed that Dixie was a barren wasteland. Atlanta's Margaret Mitchell, preparing in the twenties to write *Gone With the Wind* (1936), deeply admired North Carolina's Thomas Dixon. She loved his racist novels glorifying the Ku Klux Klan—*The Leopard's Spots* (1902), *The Klansman* (1905), and *The Traitor* (1907).

And the poet Tate shuddered upon learning that Ralph McGill, all of twenty-three years old in 1920 and destined to be the South's leading journalist, said that Mencken was "our knight in shining armor."[4]

Mencken's barbs attracted almost every reader's attention. The brighter undergraduates at the University of Virginia, the University of North Carolina at Chapel Hill, and private universities like Duke and Vanderbilt, schools hoping someday to compare themselves with Harvard or Yale, hurried each month to devour the latest issue of Mencken's *American Mercury*. Mencken's magazine, born in 1924 to succeed *The Smart Set*, was also the rage even at some of the tiny church-related schools. At North Carolina's Wake Forest College, W. J. Cash and Gerald W. Johnson first cut their teeth on Mencken and cringed whenever anyone praised Dixon or Thomas Nelson Page's sentimental novels. Dixon's nationwide popularity did little to ease their embarrassment.

But when W. D. Griffith, a transplanted Kentuckian in Hollywood, turned *The Klansman* into the first great motion picture, *Birth of a Nation* (1915), few white Southerners, even young white new liberals in the making, could help but be thrilled. Sixteen-year-old Cash saw it in 1916, "alternately bawling hysterically and shouting my fool head off." And nine-year-old Hodding Carter sat trembling in a New Orleans theater where Confederate veterans screamed the rebel yell throughout the film. President Woodrow Wilson, a Virginian and a writer, watched the film at a private showing in the White House and was said to have exulted that the film was "like writing history with lightning."[5] Griffith's cinematic masterpiece, crudely racist by today's standards, helped to give rise in 1915 to the second incarnation of the Ku Klux Klan, which flowered in the next ten years.

But was Dixie a "Sahara"? By the early twenties, intellectual magnolias and various literary flowers were blooming here and there. Little magazines with editors eager to drive a stake into the heart of the glorifiers of the "lost cause" began publication. In Virginia, Richmond's literati, clustered around Cabell, inspired by Glasgow's novels, and emboldened by Mencken's attack and encouragement, launched *The Reviewer* in 1921. Emily Clark, an editorial dynamo, published Glasgow, Mary Johnston, Mencken (crowned "King Mencken" by Cabell), and new, fresh voices: Frances Newman, Julia Peterkin, and Gerald W. Johnson. Each was a path breaker, as were others, but few could match the audacity of Georgia-born Newman's unladylike novel, *The Hard-Boiled Virgin* (1926). The Tarheel playwright Paul Green contributed to and helped edit *The Reviewer* in its last year from his professor's office in Chapel Hill, but in 1925 it withered and died for want of subscribers.

In New Orleans, the *Double Dealer* also debuted in 1921 and published new writers, including a little-known Mississippian named William Faulkner. Sojourning in New Orleans and eager to advise and guide Faulkner was Sherwood Anderson, who had come South after showing in *Winesburg, Ohio* (1919) that the North also had its share of eccentrics and haunted people. Among others, Hamilton Basso and the black author Jean Toomer published in the *Double Dealer*. The magazine limped along until it expired in 1926, but not before trying to cut the ground from under the feet of Thomas Nelson Page and others of the mint julep school of writers.

There were other signs that the beaux arts (Mencken's "Bozart") were emerging. Glasgow capped a long career with *Barren Ground* in 1925 and *The Sheltered Life* in 1932. These novels, feminist by the standards of that time, featured strong-willed, courageous women who refused to stand serenely and silently on some man-made pedestal. *Barren Ground*, with its heroine turning to work and managing a farm after she was betrayed by a man, heralded a "new woman" in the South and gave notice, as had Newman in *Dead Lovers are Faithful Lovers* (1928), that southern literature was being revitalized along gender lines. Glasgow was a major transitional figure in the intellectual history of the South, standing between the traditional, sentimental era and a new, vibrant epoch. "I do not like filling stations and smoke stacks in place of hedges," she announced in 1931. "Yet I like even less the hookworm and pellagra and lynching of the agrarian scene, the embattled forces of religious prejudice and the snarling feature of our rural dry-nurse prohibition."[6]

Starting in the 1920s, as historian George Tindall has shown, a generation of white southern novelists and scholars attempted to break free of conventional assumptions about blacks. It was a difficult task. The New South's leading lights had abhorred lynchings and race riots but confidently asserted, as Woodrow Wilson did, that they "understood" blacks, claiming that they were children at heart but capable of becoming rampaging animals. In the decades after World War I that racist assumption did not magically disappear, but several white writers attempted to examine more closely and to question racial stereotypes. One of the first was Tennessee's T. S. Stribling. His novel, *Birthright* (1922), has a black protagonist—a doctor, an educated, sensitive man, the antithesis of Dixon's shuffling black buffoons or wild-eyed rapists. Stribling reversed the Dixon formula by describing the rape of a young black girl by a white man. The book's tone and theme caused the Charlotte *News* to grumble that Mencken had obviously cast his evil spell on Stribling. In the 1930s the *News*, home to W. J. Cash and other young Southerners, identified with the emerging liberalism of writers such as Stribling.

Two South Carolinians, Julia Peterkin and DuBose Heyward, strove to create realistic black characters. They hoped to capture the black voice, to get inside a folk culture they knew to be integral to the South, but which was usually misunderstood or slandered. In her best novels, *Black April* (1927) and the Pulitzer Prize–winning *Scarlet Sister Mary* (1928), Peterkin, born in 1880, recorded the voice of South Carolina's Gullah blacks, people she had known firsthand on her family's coastal plantation. Emily Clark, one of Peterkin's champions, praised her novels in the national press.

Heyward also tried to probe the black psyche. His greatest work, *Porgy* (1925), in time became a successful play and, in the hands of George and Ira Gershwin, a classic American opera, *Porgy and Bess* (1935). Among Heyward's other works focusing on blacks and their culture, *Mamba's Daughter* (1929) was also made into a successful Broadway play, showing the North that Dixie was slowly changing. As he did with Peterkin, Mencken praised Heyward's work, but Heyward never completely shook his earlier notion that Mencken's "Sahara" was slanderous. To prove it, he and several Charlestonians formed the Poetry Society of South Carolina.

Heyward, who died at fifty-five in 1940, never matched his early successes in his later work; nor did Peterkin, who faded into obscurity long before her death in 1961. In the early 1930s Stribling wrote a sweeping historical trilogy tracing a family's fortunes from the Old South to the depression—the second volume, *The Store* (1932), won a Pulitzer Prize—but from the late thirties until his death in 1965 he contented himself with writing detective fiction.

These writers' careers suggest that they lacked the talent, the desire, or the energy to do more than take a first step beyond the Dixon-Page tradition. A similar pattern seems to characterize the career of Paul Green, the Chapel Hill poet, teacher, philosopher of sorts, editor, and playwright. In the first half of his life, Green (born in 1894) was a fearless innovator unafraid to tackle "the Negro Problem" head on by putting strong-willed, admirable blacks on stage. His courage was real. His play, *In Abraham's Bosom* (1927), at first shocked and then won over the most discerning of audiences and critics—New York City playgoers and judges. He, too, won the coveted Pulitzer Prize for his raw, truthful depiction of the lynching of his protagonist, Abraham, a mulatto, whose only sin was his color. No theater in the South would perform it.

Green audaciously invited blacks like the Missouri-born Langston Hughes to the campus of the University of North Carolina where an admirer of Hughes circulated copies of his poem, "Black Christ," with its searing line, "Christ is a nigger on the cross of the South." Green also brought Richard Wright to Chapel Hill. The two attempted to make a play of Wright's angry novel, *Native Son* (1939). In the 1930s Green worked on other plays of social realism, and he remained a conspicuous "campus liberal" for the rest of his long life. But his major creative energies in his last decades—he died in 1981—went into writing outdoor pageants, the most famous being *The Lost Colony* (1937). For well over half a century Green's "symphonic drama," as he called his pageant, has run each summer in North Carolina instructing tourists by the millions about Sir Walter Raleigh's dreams and schemes in the New World.

The white South's artistic and intellectual discovery of the black Southerner was a major effort at Chapel Hill and at other white and black schools in the years between 1920 and the Second World War. The leader among white scholars in studying and documenting black culture was Howard W. Odum. His life and achievements are ironic and paradoxical: he was a major academic figure in the post–World War I attempts to forge a new, progressive-minded South, but he could not, at the end, overcome the limitations of his background, though it was not for want of sincerity or labor. Georgia-born in 1884, he came of age imbued with New South Liberalism. He quickly emerged as one of the most prolific, important southern writers of the first half of the twentieth century.

He began studying and writing about Southerners of both races at the start of his career. In 1911, Odum published collections of African American music that became an important part of the emerging folklore movement in America. After earning doctoral degrees at both Clark and Columbia Universities, Odum taught briefly in Georgia before coming to Chapel Hill in 1920 with a mandate to build a sociology department. He established *The Journal of Social Forces* in 1922 and spread his enthusiasm for tackling the race question as creatively and as "scientifically" as possible. He and his colleague, Guy S. Johnson, collaborated to produce *The Negro and His Songs* (1925) and *Negro Workaday Songs* (1926). Their work stirred the imagination of Newman I. White in nearby Durham's new Duke University to collect and study *American Negro Folk-Songs* (1928). Odum's energy and talent even extended to writing fiction. Beginning with *Rainbow Round My*

Shoulder in 1928, Odum produced a fictional trilogy featuring his "Black Ulysses." Mencken was highly impressed. "What a trilogy!" he cried out in the *American Mercury.* "It will be read for many years."[7] The bard of Baltimore was wrong. Odum's talents as a novelist were limited, and he never overcame a tendency to romanticize black life.

Running parallel with the white discovery of the blacks' South were writings by African Americans, most of them southern born but northern based by the 1920s. Among white editors of prestigious magazines, Mencken was one of the most important publishers of black writers. African American writers who were just getting established were welcomed in the *Crisis*, the magazine of the National Association for the Advancement of Colored People (NAACP), the Urban League's *Opportunity: A Journal of Negro Life*, and the *Messenger*, a publication of the Brotherhood of Sleeping Car Porters headed by the Florida native, A. Philip Randolph. These northern publications were crucial to the artistic and intellectual development of African Americans. An outpouring of verse, fiction, history, music, and autobiography came in the 1920s. The Harlem Renaissance had begun.

Alain Locke's *The New Negro*, published in 1925, caught the wider world's attention. Its table of contents reads like a who's who of what W. E. B. Du Bois called "the Talented Tenth." Included were the novelist and activist Walter White and the poet Georgia Douglas Johnson, both graduates of Atlanta University, and Virginia's Anne Spencer, also a poet. White's *Fire in the Flint* (1924), a novel about a northern-trained black doctor who returns to his people in Georgia, helped discredit the sentimental tradition. Leaders of the Harlem Renaissance searched for identity in black folk life, all the while being acutely aware of what Du Bois, for years editor of the *Crisis*, had early on identified as the "two-ness" of being both black and American.

The centrality of a rich black culture and the sense of two-ness reverberated dynamically in the early literary efforts of James Weldon Johnson. He was a multi-talented Floridian, who moved North after passing the bar exam in Florida and founding the state's first black newspaper, *The Daily American*. All the while, he wrote poetry, fiction, history, music, and Broadway shows, the last written in collaboration with his talented brother, Rosamond. Johnson's great qualities of introspection and observation meshed perfectly with his literary talents in 1912 when he published, anonymously, *The Autobiography of an Ex-Coloured Man*. This novel—based in part on the author's life, hence the word "auto-biography" in the mysterious-sounding title—reflected Johnson's experiences as someone light enough to "pass" and thus experience the South alternately as a white and a black man. The novel's unnamed protagonist is an important precursor of Ralph Ellison's major character in *Invisible Man* (1952).

In 1927 Johnson rereleased his celebrated novel under his name and added another southern contribution to the Harlem Renaissance. That year also saw the appearance of *God's Trombones*, seven of Johnson's black sermons in verse. From 1916 to 1930 Johnson served as field secretary for the NAACP. In 1930, he became a professor at Fisk University, where he continued his social activism until his death in 1938.

Black history as a discipline came into its own during the highly creative period between the two major wars. Carter G. Woodson, a Virginian with a Harvard Ph.D., had a dream of empowering blacks by detailing the achievements of notable African Americans. He did this in *The Negro in Our History* (1922). It was not superseded until the late 1940s when John Hope Franklin wrote a fuller and more sophisticated work, *From Slavery to Freedom*. Franklin, a distinguished author of a number of books on black history, stood on the shoulders of Woodson and other black historians whose work appeared in the *Journal of Negro History*, a quarterly Woodson founded in 1916 and edited until his death in 1950.

But the South that spurred Woodson to salvage black history also produced, on the white side of the racial coin, the prodigious scholar Ulrich Bonnell Phillips. Born in Georgia in 1877, U. B. Phillips absorbed his generation's infatuation with the myth of white supremacy and the widely held view among whites (and some blacks) that one could be a progressive thinker by believing that the new Jim Crow laws protected blacks from angry whites. Phillips wrote highly influential and widely praised works of southern history. His books, *American Negro Slavery* (1918) and *Life and Labor in the Old South* (1929), were based on prodigious scholarship, but Phillips could never escape the notion that blacks were inherently inferior. After a lifetime of thinking, Phillips concluded that the resolve of the white South to keep African Americans subservient was the "Central Theme of Southern History" (1928). He may well have been right, but his positive attitude toward his argument (and his confident tone) reveals much about the man. Cash agreed with Phillips about the central theme and called its post–Civil War mentality "the savage ideal." But Cash wrote in sorrow, not with the satisfaction of the powerful.

Woodson, the father of black history, and Phillips came of age during a period of lynchings and race riots and the establishment of the Jim Crow South, an era the black historian Rayford Logan called "the nadir" of American race relations. From 1880 to 1906, some 3,500 lynchings shamed America, the vast majority (2,770) occurring in the South with blacks as the primary victims. During these twenty-six years in Mississippi an alert person would have seen or heard about a lynching on average once a month. After 1906 southern racial violence declined. But after World War I ended, the old pattern seemed to begin again. Between May and December 1919 twenty-five race riots—most but not all in the South—disgraced a nation that had just fought a great war in the name of basic human values. The official count listed five whites and twenty-five blacks dead, but many believed that a far larger number of African Americans had been killed. Would the terrible days of "the nadir" return?[8] Some blacks thought so.

What would the South's white and black intellectuals—its professors and clergymen, writers and journalists with serious intentions to think critically about social problems—do? The answer came quickly. In 1919, concerned leaders, many of them academics of the Odum variety or religious leaders, met in Atlanta to form the Commission on Interracial Cooperation (CIC). The organization sought to bring the "best" of both races together to expose and battle lynchings and improve race relations by finding ways to change the attitudes and actions of both races. The group chose Will W. Alexander, who would spend a lifetime battling for justice on many fronts, as its executive director. "Dr. Will," a freedom-minded Missourian, had studied theology at Vanderbilt and had been a Methodist army chaplain during World War I. But at war's end, Alexander dedicated his life to improving race relations by working with whites and blacks to find common grounds of understanding. Under Dr. Will's direction, the CIC threw itself into criticizing the Klan, tracking lynchings, and courting white and black leaders. In the early 1930s the CIC commissioned sociologist Arthur Raper, a passionate Chapel Hill liberal, to make a thorough study of lynchings. The result was the publication of a classic, *The Tragedy of Lynching* (1933).

Partially as a result of the information that the CIC publicized, and of the uneasiness many white Southerners were beginning to feel about the Klan's resurgence, several newspaper editors boldly criticized the Secret Order. The Klan, growing alarmingly in the early 1920s, graphically reminded Southerners that intolerance was rampant again, even if, as whites reminded themselves, the Klan's greatest popularity was in Indiana and the southwestern states. From the 1890s onwards, southern newspaper editors had routinely decried barbaric lynchings and accused demagogic politicians of inflaming the uneducated, primitive white masses. But in the 1920s the Klan's resurgence gave even the most moderate workaday journalist a target. The Klan's critics, driven by editors like Virginius Dabney of the *Richmond Times-Dispatch* and North Carolina's Gerald W. Johnson, of the *Greensboro News* and one of Mencken's proteges, "formed a loose but spirited fellowship," writes historian John Kneebone. "They studied one another's opinions, cheered colleagues under fire, and provided professional opportunities for talented young newspapermen of liberal persuasion." In 1932, Dabney surveyed *Liberalism in the South* and gave due attention to his colleagues in journalism.[9]

By the 1920s, editors and journalists, dedicated to invigorating southern journalism by adopting a more critical attitude than their successors, were writing hard-hitting editorials and graphic news accounts of lynchings and the Klan. Praise rained down from the North. Julian C. Harris of Georgia's *Columbus Enquirer Sun* (1926), Alabamian Grover C. Hall, editor of the *Montgomery Advertiser* (1928), and Louis I. Jaffe of the *Norfolk Virginian-Pilot* (1929) won Pulitzer prizes for their courageous words. Like most white Southerners, whether moderate in the manner of Odum or as deliberately liberal as Raper, the prize-winning journalists accepted the permanency of Jim Crow. But unlike the New South's pre-modernist generation who believed that whites embodied some kind of historical racial worth and inherent understanding of freedom, the writers of the 1920s "qualified the white supremacy doctrine; they now questioned the capabilities of the white masses, no matter how pure their Anglo-Saxon heritage."[10]

The sudden increase in lynchings in 1918–1919, the reemergence of the Klan, and the sporadic incidents of gruesome racism in the 1920s shocked those who in their youth had witnessed or heard lurid tales of racial barbarity. In 1918, ten-year-old Hodding Carter was wandering in some familiar woods in rural Mississippi when he came upon the charred body of a black man, another victim of "Judge Lynch." The boy vomited on the spot and was never able to expunge the awful scene from his memory. For many whites like Carter, who would one day be a prominent journalist and a voice for moderation, the violence was almost commonplace news and the perpetrators were often neighbors or acquaintances.

"One day, sometime during your childhood or adolescence," Lillian Smith wrote of her childhood in rural Georgia, "a Negro was lynched in your county or the one next to yours." Everyone knew who was responsible, "but no one publicly condemned it and always the murderers went free. And afterward, maybe weeks or months or years afterward, you sat casually in the drugstore with one of the murderers and drank the Coke he casually paid for." W. J. Cash, seeking to shock and embarrass his readers, wrote candidly in 1941 that "I have myself known university-bred men who confessed proudly to having helped roast a Negro." No New South Liberal could—or would—ever have uttered or believed such a statement.[11]

As a boy, Faulkner—whose account of the lynching-castration of Joe Christmas in *Light in August* is terrifyingly unforgettable—slept in a bedroom not far from the scene of one of the ghastliest lynchings in Mississippi's history. Historian Joel Williamson has recounted in graphic detail how young Falkner (he had not yet added the letter "u" to his name) was ten years old when his neighbors, men he knew well, dragged a black man through the streets of Oxford, "strung him up naked on a telephone pole, and riddled his body with bullets." As with many of his contemporaries, lynchings burned like acid in Faulkner's memory.[12]

For African Americans, commonplace violence burned even deeper into the soul. Young Richard Wright, a Mississippian like Faulkner and Carter, learned that his best friend's brother had been brutally murdered. A story had got about that the black man had had sex with a white prostitute. Years later Wright explored his feelings, saying that the news of lynchings brought on temporary "paralysis of will and impulse" and a sickening awareness that he and blacks were ever at risk. As long as a lynching "remained something terrible and yet remote, something whose horror and blood might descend upon me at any moment, I was compelled to give my entire imagination over to it, an act which blocked the springs of thought and feeling in me, creating a sense of distance between me and the world in which I lived."[13]

For many southern intellectuals, religious conservatism—routinely and sometimes inaccurately called "Fundamentalism"—was almost as important an issue as race by the 1920s. From the time of the Second Great Awakening of 1800–1801, the South had been a bastion of evangelical Christianity. So had the antebellum North. When many northern Protestants embraced antislavery, southern Christians turned politically conservative and, in time, religiously conservative. But Fundamentalism as a specific term describing a set of religious beliefs had originated in the North before it flowered in the South. Many Northerners were self-consciously Fundamentalists but, given the significant number of outspoken and often flamboyant southern ministers, many people came to associate the word with the South by the 1920s.

In the decade or so before the beginning of World War I, theological controversies had caused turbulence in virtually every northern denomination. To preachers and theologians of a decidedly conservative bent, the culprits were "liberals" who had fallen for "modernism." In church circles modernists believed and argued that all religious practices, doctrines, even "truths," had to be in line with the emerging social order and with facts and arguments from scientific or rational thought. For example, as northern cities grew like wildfire and produced problems such as slums, overcrowded tenements, hazardous working conditions, abandoned children, and prostitution, churches should shape their message and liturgies accordingly. Modernists argued that the "understanding" of the Bible and Christianity—indeed all religions—had evolved over time. Viewed historically, as well as sociologically, self-proclaimed modernist preachers like the renowned New Yorker, Henry Emerson Fosdick, argued that any era's cherished rites—for example, adult baptism by total immersion—need not always have been practiced in the same specific way. Fosdick shared many basic assumptions about knowledge and thinking with his counterparts in philosophy and history, from the philosopher John Dewey to the historian James Harvey Robinson. Fundamentalists often criticized the inclusion in school curricula of Robinson's acclaimed European "New History" text, *The Mind in the Making*. Debates within the religious denominations, particularly among Baptists and Presbyterians, were heated, with conservatives denouncing modernists and saying their vaunted "Higher Criticism" valued history and science more than the "absolute truths" of the Bible.

Virtually none of this often rancorous controversy infected southern churches before 1920. "In the South," writes the historian George M. Marsden, "the debates were in most cases short-lived, because dissent was simply not tolerated." Dixie's mainstream churches, mainly Baptist and Methodist, were relatively insulated by their historic conservatism—by their warm attachment to what might be called "old time religion." But when a California millionaire and others, hoping to demolish modernism in the churches, bankrolled a twelve-volume compendium of conservative Christian essays, sermons, and notes called *The Fundamentals* (1910–1915), Southerners had a big hand in the task. The first editor was a North Carolinian, Amzi C. Dixon, brother of Thomas Dixon, who had also been a Baptist minister before turning to writing racist fiction. By 1901 A. C. Dixon was a renowned Baptist evangelist and pastor of Chicago's famed Dwight L. Moody Church. There he blistered modernists and championed Fundamentalism.[14]

But the label Fundamentalism was not widely used outside religious circles until after the success of the founding of the World's Christian Fundamentals Association (WCFA) in Philadelphia in 1919. Under the leadership of Minnesota's William B. Riley, a militant foe of modernists, the new association hammered out the "Five Points" of true faith: the Bible as absolutely true; Christ's Virgin Birth; His Atonement on the cross for the world's sins; His Resurrection; and His Second Coming. By the early 1920s, after avowed Fundamentalists, North and South, had mounted a crusade to purge the churches of all modernists, the term "Fundamentalism" had made its way into the everyday vocabulary of Americans. Southerners vied with their northern brethren in energizing and popularizing Fundamentalism. A. C. Dixon was actively involved in planning the formation of the WCFA. He returned from a pastorate in England in 1920 and immediately injected his enthusiasm for extending Fundamentalist "concerns to the whole of American civilization," writes one close student of American religious history. The next two annual conferences of the WCFA were held in Raleigh, North Carolina. The 1923 conference met in Fort Worth, home of the pugnacious Baptist minister, J. Frank Norris.[15]

Southern soil in the early 1920s was particularly fertile for

Fundamentalism. The Jazz Age began almost the day the dough-boys arrived back in America after World War I. Many Southern-ers had seen worldly Paris or other places and cultures quite different from the puritanical world of their youth and their fathers and mothers. One wildly popular song caught the mood, the anxiety of the older culture: "How are you going to keep them down on the farm after they've seen Paree?" Now "hot" jazz, bathtub gin, and Flaming Youth flappers captured (and sometimes repelled) the American imagination. The twenties, as so many feared and some hoped, witnessed a revolution in man-ners and morals.

To some deeply religious believers, modernism included ev-erything the restless young seemed to favor: drinking, card play-ing, short skirts, dancing, and by the 1920s, particularly, Darwinian evolution. In 1922 the editor of one zealous Southern Baptist publication scolded President Harding for allowing "Jazz dancing" in the White House. One minister announced that adultery occurred routinely on the dance floor. While it is highly unlikely that the rural, church-dominated South saw much of "Jazz dancing," still the spread of a consumer culture fueled by newspaper advertisements and the radio brought the modern world to Dixie. As a result, "an unusual tone of urgency charac-terized ministers" and their attacks on worldliness from the early 1920s on.[16] In the post-1918 world, the South found itself on the defensive. Northerners everywhere seemed to delight in echoing that man Mencken and pointing a finger at the "benighted South." In the development of the image of the "Savage South," says Fred Hobson, "the decade of the 1920s was in many regards the most crucial decade for Southerners since the 1870s."[17]

To religious conservatives, modernism included any attempt at social reform or suggestion that the church had a duty to move beyond the gospel of personal salvation. In 1924, a prominent Tarheel minister condemned "welfare work," saying, "Show me one word in the New Testament that exhorts Christians to make the world a better place in which to live, and you may hang me from a telephone pole."[18] Yet those who agreed with such strident preachers also ardently advocated Prohibition and Sunday closing laws—two attempts at social reform, certainly. But religious conservatives—by the 1920s routinely called "Fundamentalists"—saw no contradiction between demanding that the state enforce Sunday "Blue Laws" or prohibit the teaching of evolution in the public schools and advocating the separation of church and state.

The controversy between Fundamentalists and modernists was about serious matters of how people think, what they can believe, how reason is related to faith, and how local communities should manage their schools. The issues were weighty and many men and women—sincere, good, and true—tried to think through the controversies in a calm, rational manner. But religious zealots and cynical caustic critics like H. L. Mencken made the religious and social issues seem narrow and irrational. At this moment, Fundamentalists decided to train their biggest guns on Darwinism, namely the teaching of evolution in the schools. There was an inner if perhaps unconscious logic behind the narrowing of the religious debate to the focus on evolution. As historian Willard Gatewood has written, "fundamentalist leaders came to recognize evolution as an issue that would enable them to reach a mass audience and rally to their cause those who professed little interest in, or understanding of, the doctrinal concerns emphasized in various sets of statements known as 'the fundamentals.' "[19]

"By the process through which complex problems become simplified," historian George Tindall observed, "the defense of faith . . ." came down to one issue "and [depended] upon the peerless leadership of William Jennings Bryan."[20]

Bryan, the "Great Commoner" from Nebraska who had retired to Florida and made a goodly sum of money brokering real estate, was immensely popular in rural America as a lay preacher. Many Southerners considered him one of the saintliest men in America. When he announced that the teaching of Darwinian evolution would result in atheism and total ruin for the country, many Fundamentalists listened and cheered him on. Bryan took his message to Virginia and Wisconsin but failed to generate sufficient interest among politicians. In South Carolina in 1921 the upper house agreed with him that teaching evolution was a crime, but the lower house said no.

The following year Bryan stumped Kentucky denouncing the "Enemies of the Bible." But an anti-evolution bill failed to pass in the lower house by one vote, thanks in part to the outspoken opposition of the state university president and several key newspaper editors. The jubilant editor of the Louisville *Evening Post* felt Kentucky had a right to boast: "We were the first to fight this thing through on behalf of modernity and we won."

In 1923 Bryan delivered a passionate exhortation to Georgia's House of Representatives to outlaw Darwin's teachings in the schools. One Bryanite declared: "Read the Bible. It teaches you how to act. Read the hymnbook. It contains the finest poetry ever written. Read the almanac. It shows you how to figure out what the weather will be. There isn't another book that is necessary for anyone to read." But Bryan's proposals never even made it to a legislative vote, thanks in part to the crusading opposition of Julian Harris's editorials in the Columbus *Enquirer-Sun*.[21]

Oklahoma enacted anti-evolution legislation in 1923. But Florida's lawmakers, although allowing Bryan to address its two houses and write the text of a proposed law, limited their action to a joint resolution against the teaching of atheism or the Darwinian theory as "fact." Bryan and Fundamentalism had lots of friends and admirers in Mississippi, Tennessee, Texas, Louisiana, and North Carolina. In varying degrees, all five states considered the issue of Darwinism in the schools.

The various factions in the squabble over evolution in the South was played out in fascinating detail in North Carolina. For years the Tarheel state had prided itself on being more enlightened and progressive than its neighbors. North Carolinians liked to say that their state was a valley of humility between two mountains of conceit, Virginia and South Carolina. The adage does not rise much above an inoffensive, playful phrase, but many national Fundamentalist leaders looked upon North Carolina as both progressive and pious, home to a large number of Baptist evangelical churches, and therefore an excellent choice for a full-scale battle. In the University of North Carolina the state boasted a school led by administrators determined to make advancements in every academic endeavor. Yet the Klan had a significant following in North Carolina. In 1921 William J. Simmons, Imperial Wizard of the Secret Order, conducted a series of well-publicized and well-attended rallies across North Carolina and spoke before a throng of two thousand in Raleigh's Baptist Tabernacle. The state's Superior Court was headed by Henry Grady, a Klansman. If Tarheel evolutionists (or modernists) could be routed, purged from the schools, the churches, and the government, a symbolic victory would have been won, paving the way for success across the land.[22]

Colorful evangelists stormed the Tarheel state, touching off revivals everywhere. Among the leaders dedicated to conquering North Carolina were A. C. Dixon and Thomas T. Martin of Blue Mound, Mississippi. They called the latter "Hell in the High Schools" Martin because of his polemical book attacking the schools. Also preaching was Baxter McLendon (popularly known as "Cyclone Mack") and the equally sensational Mordecai F. Ham of Kentucky. With the Tarheel state blaring with anti-evolution sermons and, in some remote places, blazing brightly with the fires of camp meetings and tent revivals, anti-evolutionists trained their guns on Dr. William Louis Poteat, president of Wake Forest College. This was a Baptist school, but Poteat, a scientist and believing Baptist, announced that he saw no conflict between science and religion, and said a person could both be a Christian and believe in evolution. To Billy Sunday, the Hams, and the Cyclone Macks, Poteat's utterances were infuriating. It was one thing for aggressive agnostics like Mencken to praise evolution—they were lost souls. But to men like Sunday the truly dangerous foes were popular, pious men like Poteat. He had obviously been duped by the evolutionists. No wonder Mencken admired Poteat, who was a European-trained biologist and devoted Sunday school teacher, and called him the "liaison officer between the Baptist revelation and human progress."[23]

A. C. Dixon, back from having served as a pastor at a prestigious Baptist church in London, came to Wake Forest and denounced the president and his views in a commencement address in 1920. Keenly watching it all was W. J. Cash, an undergraduate who worshipped Poteat and despised what Dixon said and the cause he represented. Cash and the Dixon brothers, Amzi and Thomas, were natives of Shelby, North Carolina, but the similarities stopped there as Cash made clear in the college newspaper.

Poteat's admirers, many of whom were Baptist ministers, stood by him like a rock. Leading the defense was the Winston-Salem journalist, Gerald W. Johnson, who constantly berated Dixon, Martin, and the other anti-evolutionists. In this he was aided by his father, Archibald Johnson, editor of the religious magazine, *Charity and Children,* and his uncle, Livingston Johnson, who edited the influential Baptist publication, the *Biblical Recorder,* both of whom were outspoken Baptist Fundamentalists. But like Poteat they saw no catastrophe in joining evolution with Christianity. All three of the Johnsons were pro-Poteat from the start and aimed their fire at the Hams, the Macks, and the other anti-evolution zealots.

In the midst of the warfare over Poteat and Wake Forest, the trustees were besieged by forces from both sides. The anti-evolutionists were the most vocal, often abusive, and sometimes downright silly. Perhaps the zaniest was one Charles F. Bluske, who publicly challenged Poteat and any three other scientists to meet him in a boxing ring. He promised to knock out all four in less than two minutes, "proving to the Public that Scientists are weak in mind and body." Poteat politely ignored pugilist Bluske and his other critics, always remaining calm and good humored. He remained confident that the majority of Tarheel Baptists were sensible and fair in their judgments. Many critics abused him without stint, but the trustees of Wake Forest stood firm and unanimously backed their embattled president in 1922. Later, when Cash penned his famous book, *The Mind of the South* (1941), he lauded Poteat as a genuine hero and heaped abuse on the Dixons and their followers.

Unable to dislodge Poteat or ruin his reputation, the fire-brands among the anti-evolutionists stepped up their criticisms of Darwinism and other attacks on the schools. They turned to the politicians and demanded legislation making it a crime to teach evolution and any modernist ideas in the public schools. William Jennings Bryan, a folk hero to religious Tarheels and three times the Democratic Party's presidential nominee, arrived from the north in 1923 for a round of speeches and sermons designed to put muscle in the arms of Christian legislators. So did Mordecai Ham, who preached his anti-evolution sermon in the state to thousands of Tarheels, many of whom heard it more than once. "The usual conclusion to his 'evolution sermon,' " says Willard Gatewood, "was his frequently repeated warning: 'The day is not distant when you will be in the grip of the Red Terror and your children will be taught free love by the damnable theory of evolution.' "[24]

Ham's radicalism often included anti-Semitic diatribes, which reached a new high of irrationality in 1924 when he publicly accused Julius Rosenwald, a Chicago millionaire whose philanthropy had greatly aided the South, of being involved in vice, prostitution, and white slavery. The editor of the Elizabeth City *Independent* so pointedly denounced Ham's charges—saying that he was a demagogue "gifted in 'the art of making people hate' "—that Ham left the state for a while until the controversy had cooled down. Billy Sunday, America's most renowned preacher, came to rally Christians in North Carolina, and in 1923 the state's governor, lobbied by a powerful chapter of the Daughters of the Confederacy, began denouncing evolutionists.[25]

To the surprise of those who think that the South was of one simple monolithic mind—an impression conveyed by *The Mind of the South* for all of Cash's worship of Poteat and praise for Chase and his allies—the great majority of Tarheel newspapers lined up against the anti-evolutionists. The forces standing against the Fundamentalist zealots in the legislature were led by the president of the University of North Carolina, Harry W. Chase, a Northerner who was trying to make the university into a first-class school. He was eloquent and forceful in his defense of freedom of speech. That and his general reputation for fairness won support from many quarters.

During the most heated days of the war of words, Nell Battle Lewis, columnist for the Raleigh *News and Observer,* rivaled Mencken in defending Poteat and Chase. She routinely abused their critics. She was convinced that most people were ignorant of Darwinism, knowing only that it was evil because the zealots said so. Lewis ran a weekly quiz on evolution during the controversy and awarded a copy of Hendrick von Loon's book, *Toleration,* to each week's winner. Lewis, Chase, and the Poteats won the last round. In 1926 the state legislature defeated an anti-evolution bill by a sizable margin.

Back came Ham, "Cyclone Mack," and Sunday armed with their Bibles and deeply held convictions. But their crowds dwindled. Cash watched it all closely from his lowly post as a Carolina high school teacher. Later, when he published *The Mind of the South,* he heaped criticism on the proponents of the legislation and praised Lewis, Chase, and all who fought for freedom of thought. Here were people "of native good sense and good will" who represented the South at its best.

The war in North Carolina was abruptly eclipsed in mid-1925 as the nation turned its attention to the tiny hamlet of Dayton. In July in the town of Dayton, in southeastern Tennessee, John T. Scopes went on trial for breaking the state's new Butler Act, a law banning the teaching of Darwinism in the public schools. Scopes was a young, likeable high school biology teacher. When asked by several town boosters, who thought a showcase trial on the teaching of evolution would put sleepy Dayton on the map, Scopes amiably agreed to do his part and get arrested. The town perpetrators had heard that the national American Civil Liberties Union was looking for a case to test the constitutionality of anti-evolution legislation. The ACLU was deadly serious; the town boosters thought the whole thing would be "a bit of a lark" and help business. Young Scopes and Dayton had no inkling of the storm they were about to unleash. Scopes was arrested and charged with violating the law. The "Monkey Trial," as many in the press would begin calling it, turned into a media circus with live, national radio coverage of the proceedings and H. L. Mencken and scores of reporters from around the world covering the trial. The defense team consisted of three celebrated northern attorneys, headed by the famous Clarence Darrow, who had just won renewed national celebrity by saving the lives of the young Chicago thrill killers, Leopold and Loeb, by invoking the insanity defense. Somewhat to the annoyance of the state's prosecutors, in came William Jennings Bryan to assist and finally take over the case for the prosecution. Both sides took the case seriously, believing (rightly) that highly important issues were on trial. Bryan yearned for a victory; he was convinced that Christian faith was being undermined.[26]

After a six-day trial, Scopes was convicted and ordered to pay a small fine. Most Daytonians reacted to the trial and to Darrow with equanimity. But the defenders of faith were outraged at Darrow's cross-examination of Bryan and by the minimal "slap on the wrist" Scopes received from the judge. Bryan, already ill before the trial, collapsed and died in Dayton within a week of its conclusion.

Dayton, for all its cultural and intellectual isolation, was hardly a Fundamentalist enclave, but Mencken's lurid portrayals of the locals as Bible-thumping yokels thirsty for the blood of any freethinker shaped the way the whole affair would be viewed for generations. Mencken was not alone in his eagerness to portray Daytonians as rustic hillbillies, but his torrent of colorful abuse shaped the thinking of several generations of historians and writers. The highly successful play and film, *Inherit the Wind,* reflected Mencken's views, often to the detriment of the facts. Most historians have believed that Darrow humiliated Bryan and helped bring on his death and that the trial symbolized and signaled the failure of Fundamentalism for the next several generations.

But the Yankees did not attack the South without reason. Dixie boasted its share of evangelists and preachers who could mesmerize their followers with vivid word pictures of a degener-

ate society bound for hellfire. One of the most prominent was
the pugnacious Texan, J. Frank Norris, minister of a large Baptist
church in Dallas. His overwrought pronouncements and actions
made him irresistible to journalists and critics of the Fundamentalists. He carried a firearm, he bragged, in case some of Satan's
followers should attempt to harm him in any way. When Norris
suspected that someone had tampered with the wiring of his radio
station, he thundered: "Some of you low down devils that monkey around this property, arrange for your undertaker before you
come around here." Nationally, Norris was a fringe member of
the anti-evolutionist crusade, but he was "the leading fundamentalist organizer in Texas, and had already won such notoriety
among his fellow Southern Baptists that he had been successfully
banned from local, county, and state organizations."[27] But Norris
continued fighting and defaming his enemies. He once advertised
that he would preach against "the ten biggest devils in Ft. Worth,
names given." When he verbally abused the Roman Catholic
mayor of the city, one of the mayor's friends accosted Norris,
who promptly shot and killed him on the spot. The jury acquitted
Norris, citing self-defense, but the incident helped to discredit
Fundamentalism even further.[28]

To many of the South's intellectuals the circus atmosphere in
Dayton was an embarrassment. Liberals lauded Darrow and tried
to popularize his argument that the trial was really about close-
mindedness versus intellectual freedom. In *The Advancing South*,
an embarrassed Mims argued with passion that Bryan and the
combative Fundamentalists did not represent the majority of
southern Christians. He praised New York City's Henry Emerson
Fosdick, the bête noire of all leading Fundamentalists, North Carolina's Baptist Henry Louis Poteat, and theological liberals everywhere. In his own denomination, Southern Methodism, Mims
announced that "the liberals are growing in number and influence
each year," a fact he believed to be true of all the mainline
churches in the South. He noted approvingly that Douglas Free-
man, editor of the Richmond, Virginia, *News-Leader*, agreed with
him that Bryan had vastly overreached himself when he had said

during the trial that "the contest between evolution and Christianity is a duel to the death."[29]

Had he lived to read Mims's strictures, Bryan would not have been surprised. Starting in the 1890s Vanderbilt's president, James H. Kirkland, had led a long, often acrimonious academic and then legal battle to free the university from the control of the Methodist Church. In 1914 Tennessee's highest court ruled in Vanderbilt's favor, prompting Virginius Dabney, a staunch foe of the anti-evolutionists, to gloat in *Liberalism in the South* (1932) that the university was allowed "to go forward under Chancellor Kirkland instead of backward with the Methodist church." No wonder Bryan had called Vanderbilt "the center of Modernism in the South." At the conclusion of the Scopes Trial Kirkland announced that "the answer to the episode at Dayton is the building of new laboratories on the Vanderbilt campus for the teaching of science." Radical fundamentalists were angry at Mencken and disappointed when only two other states—Mississippi (1926) and Arkansas (1928)—passed anti-evolution laws.[30]

But had evolution won the hearts and minds of the South? "Even Southerners who questioned the propriety of anti-evolution legislation were likely to be hostile to Darwin's theory," concluded a careful historian. And Cash argued that the forces against evolution constituted "an authentic folk movement" that transcended mere legislation.[31]

The entrenched anti-modernist impulse inherent in Fundamentalism continues to undergird the fight against evolution even today. After Scopes, Norris, described by one liberal northern church magazine as "probably the most belligerent fundamentalist now abroad in the land," attacked evolution for the next thirty years. So, too, did Ham, who railed that evolution leads to Communism and reviled Darwinism as the "Red Flag of Bolshevism" until his death in 1961. Along the way in 1934 he converted a sixteen-year-old North Carolinian named Billy Graham. By the early 1950s, Graham would moderate his pronouncements, move well beyond the crude rhetoric of Norris and Ham, and rise to be America's most celebrated evangelist.[32]

On the question of evolution, Ham, Graham, Norris, Billy Sunday, and Cyclone Mack accomplished what the law could not—the intimidation or conversion of southern public opinion. For decades after Scopes, teachers in both public and private schools often shied away from direct comments about evolution or Darwin. In 1946, when a Mississippi college student purchased her Western Civilization text, the clerk ripped out the pages devoted to Darwin. In 1960 an investigator who had covered the Scopes Trial reported that no Tennessee teachers remained employed if they openly taught or mentioned evolution approvingly.

The Scopes Trial also contributed to a serious reaction among a group of young Southerners who had begun speaking their minds in 1920. That year at Vanderbilt University several professors and students—aspiring poets, all—gathered together to talk about literature, poetry mainly. Led by young English professors John Crowe Ransom and Donald Davidson and, from 1921, by a precocious undergraduate, Allen Tate, who was given to quoting T. S. Eliot and other modernist poets, the group began publishing *The Fugitive*. In time, others, notably Robert ("Red") Penn Warren, a shy, redheaded undergraduate from Kentucky, joined the discussions and contributed verses. The "Fugitives," as many would come to call them, were of many minds about social issues, but they were united in their rejection of both a sentimental yearning for the "lost cause" and the New South optimism of the head of the English Department, Edwin Mims. Mims, while hardly hostile to the young men, did try to discourage their foray into print; he was a proponent of moralistic, uplifting verse. Neither Mims nor the Vanderbilt administration did anything to help the fledgling publication, but when the poets Ransom and Tate attracted national praise, Mims and other university officials sought to bask in the limelight.

The Fugitive, for all its acclaim, folded after nineteen issues, just months after the Scopes Trial concluded. By then, the Fugitives were no longer a coherent group. Some, like Tate, who yearned to be a citizen of the world, had moved North and had cultivated New York friends, many of whom were decidedly liberal and given to sharing Mencken's view of the South. But Ransom and Davidson, particularly bothered by the carnival atmosphere at Dayton and deeply critical of Mims's liberal reaction to the trial, decided it was time to regroup intellectually and find a way to defend the South against the charges of Mencken and much of the national press. Among his comrades in arms, Davidson fumed at Mencken but he prudently waited until 1928 to publish a more restrained response in a national magazine.

By 1926 Ransom, Davidson, and Tate, who now yearned to fashion a southern identity, began talking about how best to frame their views. By this time, the three men, joined by several Vanderbilt professors of English, history, and psychology, decided it was time to come together intellectually and attack the Menckens and Darrows and the Mimses of the day. Several of the original Fugitives had stayed in touch and refined their ideas, and many were, in varying degrees, still hostile to what they considered the materialistic, impersonal world of machines and smokestacks and the worship of progress.

From Vanderbilt the invitations went out to several other distinguished writers, including "Red" Warren, to submit essays for a volume that would, as Ransom stressed, "support a Southern way of life against what might be called the American or prevailing way." From the start it was clear "that the best terms in which to represent the distinction are contained in the phrase, Agrarian versus Industrial." The result was the publication in 1930 of *I'll Take My Stand* by "Twelve Southerners."[33]

With varying degrees of insight and style, the Agrarians, Davidson, Ransom, Tate, and Warren (the four former Fugitives who were committed to the cause and the book) and their eight protégés and colleagues all attempted to speak to some issue that was, in their minds, particularly southern. While the book lacked any cohesive unity or common view—the twelve authors wrote highly personal pieces—their essays revolved around four themes: family, place, leisure, and religion.[34]

In many ways, the book was a search for values, a quest flowing from a heartfelt concern that the souls of men and women were being lost or destroyed by modernity, here meaning machines, cities, displacement from the land, or other human beings. Spirituality, defined broadly, was not far from the center of several essays, though only Tate addressed the issue head on in his "Remarks on Southern Religion," a penetrating essay. Like Ransom, Tate was at the beginning of an intellectual search for a religious certainty an intellectual could defend—a faith Tate would find in 1950 when he formally converted to Roman Catholicism.

But for all of their genuine, often eloquent, concern about and love of their region the Twelve Southerners assumed that "the South" was a white man's country and all but ignored African Americans except as a "problem" for whites. Only Warren, one of the youngest of the group (only twenty-five in 1930), addressed the issue head on—and he was ambivalent about dealing with the subject. He did not share the vehement feelings of the others—particularly Donald Davidson's fierce attachment to segregation—and he accepted his assignment reluctantly.[35] He was away in England with his mind on literature, but he hurriedly whipped off "The Briar Patch," a call for blacks to succeed by being allowed to work the land and for whites to treat them fairly, as long as social inequality was not breached. In this, Warren virtually repeated the paternalism of Edwin Mims and New South Liberals. But even these words of moderation—and Warren admitted years later that "The Briar Patch" was a defense of Jim Crow—angered the archconservative Donald Davidson who objected strongly to the inclusion of Warren's essay.

I'll Take My Stand touched off considerable controversy with reviewers and readers (and still does even today) who tend to latch on to specific ideas and to ignore the rest. But what did the agrarian manifesto accomplish? Not much beyond gaining the undying admiration of various literary people and a few converts like Richard Weaver, who would later emerge as a perceptive social conservative. Agrarianism had no influence on policy makers at any level. The idea, while often beautifully expressed, ignored race and lacked enough coherence to establish a school of thinkers. Critics at the time and since have found it difficult to be neutral about the Fugitive-Agrarians and their near glorification of a nonexistent past. Some prize Agrarianism as an early example of concern about the environment; others treasure the group's warnings against the impersonality of corporate capitalism. One of their harsher critics, John Egerton, in his recent, wide-ranging, important study of this era has said, "By indirection and by determined avoidance of an overtly reactionary motive, the organizers of the Agrarian rebellion thus challenged an enemy they couldn't defeat with an ideal they couldn't defend. . . ."[36]

According to Cash, who has often been accused of being too critical of the South, Tate and company may have failed to see any defects in the Old South and were the "spiritual heirs of Thomas Nelson Page," but it "is probably fair to say that this has been well balanced out by their services in puncturing the smugness of Progress, in directing attention to the evils of laissez-faire industrialism, . . . and in recalling that the South must not be too much weaned away from its ancient leisureliness—the assumption that the first end of life is living itself—which, as they rightly contend, is surely one of its greatest virtues."[37]

THE SOUTHERN RENAISSANCE

To most Southerners in 1930 and throughout the following decade the views of the "Twelve Southerners" could not have been more irrelevant. The stock market collapse of 1929 and the decade-long depression seared the region. Unemployment was now the enemy, along with hunger and hopelessness and tin-roof shacks—one jazz artist memorialized the problem in "Tin Roof Blues"—and not some abstract "industrialism." Food and jobs were needed far more than some romanticized pastoral South. Early in the thirties, southern textile mills, Dixie's main industry after agriculture, shut their doors or limped along offering a few hours of work per week. Southern agriculture, while having in 1922 rebounded to some extent from the economic woes following 1918, sank further into decay. By the end of the depression decade, southern sharecroppers and tenants, black and white, were living in shocking poverty.

The poverty in the South was worse than that in the North. The South had shared only minimally in the ballyhooed national prosperity of the 1920s. But what would Dixie's wordsmiths say about the impact of the depression? What should they do? Agrarianism proved to be no answer, particularly since its authors— ridiculed by some as the "Twelve Confederates"—scattered, and turned their attentions to a host of unrelated issues. Remnants of the Agrarians regrouped in 1938 to publish *Who Owns America?* This second declaration, edited by a new recruit from Kentucky, Herbert Agar, lacked the punch and stylistic polish of *I'll Take My Stand*.

Did politicians have the answers? To intellectuals, whether Chapel Hill liberal or Vanderbilt conservative, the question was not even worth asking, given the lack of politicians with any national standing or reputation. Intellectuals had not looked to politicians for meaningful leadership since the days of slavery. Before 1914 New South advocates had hoped to influence politics but had done so with a faint heart given the prominence of racist rabble-rousers like "Pitchfork" Ben Tillman and "Coley" Blease of South Carolina or Mississippi's James K. Vardaman. Vardaman's demagoguery was symbolized all too clearly in his defeat of the Delta patrician, LeRoy Percy, in 1911. Thirty years later LeRoy's son, William Alexander Percy, would warn the world about the revolt of the Mississippi masses in *Lanterns on the Levee* (1941). True, Woodrow Wilson was a Virginian, but many of Dixie's politicians of national prominence were openly, crudely racist and thus were part of the problem, not the solution.

As a result of all this, and given the nature of intellectual life in the South, there had been no tradition of ideological debate since antebellum days. Nor did the modern South have political philosophers comparable to John Dewey or Walter Lippmann in the North. The closest southern intellectuals came to thinking programmatically—and departing from the New South Liberals' fondness for praising moral leadership—was the Agrarians' vague enthusiasm for persuading people to treasure the land and small farms.

Intellectuals also shared (sometimes more than they knew) in their region's long-held affection for states' rights and suspicion of the federal government. But the issue went deeper. The South's major problems—Jim Crow, support of the Klan, violence, and an anti-intellectual religious Fundamentalism—seemed rooted in its unique history and culture of slavery, the defeat in the Civil War, and the lingering anger over Reconstruction. Many intellectuals assumed with Cash that "the South is another land"—American in many ways but, at bottom, different from the rest of the nation.

So it is hardly surprising that very few Southerners in the 1930s made a radical or even moderate turn to the left—to calls for socialism or for the rudiments of the welfare state. Unlike some prominent northern intellectuals who were mesmerized for a while by Marxism, Southerners with rare exceptions were immune to the blandishments of any left-wing ideology or utopian ideas about creating a classless state and relegating religion to being the opium of the people. Among Southerners of any standing only Richard Wright (who joined the Communist Party after moving to Chicago) would have ever considered writing "agit-prop" (agitation and propaganda) literature. True, the highly publicized 1929 textile strike at Gastonia, North Carolina, prompted the writing of several mostly forgettable Marxist or "proletarian" novels, the best being Olive Tilford Dargan's *Call Home the Heart* (1932), written under the nom de plume Fielding Burke, and Grace Lumpkin's *To Make My Bread* (1932). Otherwise, the South produced no one comparable, say, to New York dramatist Clifford Odets, author of *Waiting for Lefty.*

Most Southerners of intellectual or literary prominence counted themselves moderates, perhaps "liberal"—which in the South meant openly opposing the excesses of racism but condoning racial segregation or "social equality" as some put it—and voted routinely for Franklin Roosevelt. He was a Democrat, after all, and far more economically and socially conservative than his detractors could see. During this era, self-proclaimed southern Republicans of any prominence were rare, except in Appalachia.

John Egerton has written that by 1932, when the depression had driven hard times even deeper into southern life and FDR was confidently promising a New Deal, the South was desperate for leadership. Few of its thinkers were avid New Dealers, and their number grew fewer yet after the New Deal's slight swing to the left in 1935–1936—proposing such measures as Social Security, extensive work relief, the National Labor Relations Act, and the Rural Electrification Administration. When FDR attempted to "pack" the Supreme Court in 1937, and in the following year tried to purge the party of certain prominent Dixie Democrats, more southern thinkers became deeply suspicious of him.[38]

But in truth the hurly-burly of politics, especially when represented by demagogues such as Louisiana's Huey Long, had never had much attraction for southern intellectuals. Instead they concentrated their attention on probing and sometimes exposing the cruelties of their region's folk culture.

For a while and for some people, ideas clustered around the concept of "Regionalism" shone brightly in the intellectual firmament. Regionalism sprang mainly from the fertile mind of Carolina's Howard W. Odum. He was an inspiration to many social scientists at Chapel Hill and across the South. Odum turned out book upon book (twenty in all) and hundreds of articles, speeches, and reviews. Deeply earnest, he exuded idealism and radiated a hopeful attitude toward every social problem, even the thorny race issue.

In reflection of these attitudes, Odum founded the Institute for Research in Social Science and *The Journal of Social Forces* at Chapel Hill. Odum's colleagues and disciples—and his presence at the university attracted scores of talented social scientists—published in the journal and helped make it a major outlet for liberals throughout the nation. He worked tirelessly until his death in 1954. He gently but firmly and successfully twisted the arms of northern philanthropists to bankroll detailed studies of southern economic conditions, the status of labor relations, the region's embryonic welfare programs and, of course, the race question. Northerners with deep pockets underwrote countless programs championed by Odum, from his desire to improve prison conditions to his life-long passion for the South's dairy industry to his New South dream of agricultural diversification.

By the late 1920s Odum had subsumed his various causes under the heading of Regionalism. The idea was forward-looking and positive, reflecting Odum's conviction that the South had to be understood and improved as a region. Odum pointedly disavowed Sectionalism, long the bane of the South in his mind. Part of Regionalism's appeal was that in looking forward it seemed to be an intelligent alternative to Agrarianism. In Odum's hands, Regionalism would spur the gathering of information—facts, statistics, folklore—and thereby lay an informed basis for intelligent planning for a brighter future. Tradition was not to be despised, but nothing must be allowed to stand in the way of ordered progress.

The Chapel Hill Regionalists produced studies of major significance to anyone trying to understand the South. *The Journal of Social Forces* bulged with factual articles on child labor, mill conditions, prisons, schools, farms, and factories. Odum planned and edited *Southern Pioneers in Social Interpretation* (1925) with its eulogistic portrayal of Walter Hines Page and other New South worthies. In 1929 Odum's disciple, Rupert B. Vance, produced the first landmark work in Regionalism, *Human Factors in Cotton Culture*. The next year, Odum published *An American Epoch: Southern Portraiture in the National Picture*, an imaginative probing of four generations of folk culture. In 1932 Vance completed his *Human Geography of the South*, a work George Tindall has called "an exhaustive guide to the Southern scene at that time."[39]

The ever-energetic Odum oversaw various sociological investigations which he turned into a big influential work—the massive, wide-ranging, richly detailed book, *Southern Regions of the United States* (1936). Dividing the United States into six regions, Odum gave his primary attention to the Southeast (the ten

Confederate states save Texas) and argued that since it was the poorest and most underdeveloped region it stood first in line for Odum's proposed federal planning group. Odum saw many Souths in the Southeast—the black belt, Appalachia, the Delta, the piney woods and forest sections, and, of course, his own area, the Piedmont. Odum firmly believed that while the South seemed peculiar and wedded to the past, there was a "silent South" of concerned Southerners who wanted to look away from the past with its romantic attachment to Sectionalism, to being different from the rest of the country, and toward the future.[40]

On a readability scale Odum's opus scored a low grade— even his greatest admirers had to turn often to caffeine to stay awake reading it—but it summed up, both in its scope and its argument, the essence of Regionalism—a future-oriented South led by social scientists planning with care and working hand in glove with government, educational and scientific institutions, and private industry. The Vanderbilt Agrarian, Donald Davidson, horrified by social science and social planning, tried to destroy the impact of Odum's book by saying it was antithetical to "our history." But moderate and liberal intellectuals across the South applauded Odum's achievement. Gerald W. Johnson proposed "capital punishment for every [southern] newspaper reporter who could not prove within a specified time" that he had read Odum's opus and the other works of the Chapel Hill Regionalists.[41]

A New Deal official in Atlanta helped persuade FDR to commission a thorough study and exposure of southern conditions. The resulting work, the *Report on Economic Conditions of the South* (1938), documented Odum's contentions: Southerners ranked at the bottom on any social and economic scale and the region's natural resources were being under-utilized or squandered. Conservative politicians and not a few other apologists said this was not true; that Yankees were up to their old trick of smearing the South. But the report had been put together by Southerners and rested heavily on the work of Odum and the Regionalists.

Odum and his colleagues had relied greatly on northern philanthropy—and would continue to do so as Odum tried to put his ideas into action. He had in mind a Council on Southern Regional Development. In 1938 southern academics, businessmen, labor leaders, and journalists responded to Odum's call for a meeting in Atlanta where Odum's ambitious ideas for a far-reaching council with a long-range plan were presented. But Odum's grand scheme was stalled and then killed by competing groups such as the soon-to-be-established Southern Conference on Human Welfare—discussed more fully in the following essay. Even though Frank Porter Graham, the well-known liberal president of the University of North Carolina, attended SCHW meetings and served as its first president, Odum kept his distance from what he considered a rival to his plans for a dynamic regional planning organization.

The Chapel Hill planner was greatly disappointed. But he went on writing and planning and trying to gain converts to Regionalism. In 1942–1943 the leadership of the Council on Interracial Cooperation concluded that their organization had become tepid and out of date. Will Alexander proposed that the CIC disband and be replaced with a group along the lines of Odum's idea of a Council on Southern Regional Development. In February 1944 "Dr. Will" and other CIC officials voted to disband the CIC and form the Southern Regional Council (SRC). Odum was elected to head the new interracial group.

Today, it is hard to remember how brightly Howard Odum's star once blazed. Professors read or try to read his books, but few others do. Why, or what, caused the almost total eclipse of his reputation? First, there were others in his day—Faulkner, Cash, Woodward, and many more—who wrote better and thought more deeply than he did. Second, Regionalism seemed to be a vital idea and Regionalists produced some seminal studies, but the idea itself turned out to be long on soaring ideals but short on real prescriptions. Richard King has written, perhaps with too much acidity, that Odum's passion for Regionalism "resembled a sort of vulgar Marxism. Once economic problems had been solved, racial and class conflicts would disappear."[42]

Then, too, on the omnipresent issue of race, the question

that would come to dominate much of the thought during the second half of the twentieth century, Odum was mired in the New South paternalism of his youth, an attitude which rendered him incapable of accepting the sea change that would come to race relations. By 1946, dissenters like Lillian Smith were criticizing the SRC's unwillingness even to discuss abandoning Jim Crow. Privately, Odum complained that he wished his friends would just shut up about Jim Crow and make Regionalism work. But Odum was now out of date; to his critics no interracial group could "go to work" within a context of racial segregation. In 1946 Odum angrily resigned as president and quit the SRC. By the time of his death eight years later, his great reputation as a thinker had all but disappeared.

But among Odum's contemporaries there were Southerners—black and white, male and female—who produced a body of work from the mid-1920s through the early 1940s that was often the stuff of genius and would in time be recognized as comprising a literary renaissance whose influence is still being felt. This renaissance reached a high water mark in 1929 with the appearance of William Faulkner's two novels, *Sartoris* (later to be titled *Flags in the Dust*) and *The Sound and the Fury*. These highly complex, brilliant books explored the human condition as no Southerner had before. Particularly in *The Sound and the Fury*, in which the three widely different Compson brothers, including the slobbering Benjy who is severely retarded, and their sister, the promiscuous Candance who cannot resist the incestuous desires of her brother Quentin, was a modernist masterpiece. Its rapid shifting back and forth in time, its murky, quirky style, its cast of extremely complex characters—Candance names her baby girl Quentin, after her brother Quentin who kills himself—and its extreme subtlety overwhelmed most critics, who could not fully appreciate Faulkner's stunning achievement. His next book, *As I Lay Dying* (1930), met the same shocked outrage—and low sales.

Hurt, somewhat bewildered—and Faulkner was a proud man, a powerhouse of ambition to be a great writer and to be appreciated by both critics and cash-paying customers—Faulkner thumbed his nose at the critics and gave the public what it wanted, in *Sanctuary* (1931). This is a Gothic novel of nymphomania, of bestial physical and racial violence, including a gruesome rape. Yet it contains some of Faulkner's finest writing. The horrified critics did not think so. They shook a stern, disapproving finger at the book's "pornography." One highly placed northern critic complained that every page was "a calculated assault on one's sense of the normal."[43]

But *Sanctuary* sold, and sold well, allowing Faulkner to return to writing what were clearly his heart's darlings. First came *Light in August* (1932), the haunting tale of Joe Christmas, a confused, primitive man who thought he must be black—the reader never really learns—forced to live in a violent society mired in the past, imprisoned in irrational hatred. Four years later came *Absalom, Absalom!* (1936), a brilliant exploration of the conjunction of history, sex, and race. As in his earlier novels and his last great works, *Go Down Moses* (1942) and *Intruder in the Dust* (1947)—another riveting story centered around white racism and lynching—Faulkner rooted his characters in time and place and revealed the powerful grip of history.

Here was a new, powerful voice, one that called out deeper feelings and probed life in a way that few readers or critics were willing to confront. Faulkner's scrambling of time and syntax, his stream-of-consciousness style, his love of arcane words, his realism, his creation of failed men and the need for honor and community were too new, too raw and disturbing. His major characters, as Cleanth Brooks has observed, are failed romantic-idealists, alienated men who have never grown up—doubtless emblematic of the defeated post–Civil War South.[44] Most critics, overwhelmed by Faulkner's style and density of thought, dismissed him as a decadent, his novels wallowing in immorality and depravity.

By the end of World War II Faulkner's books were limping along in sales or had to be searched for in second-hand bookstores. Then in 1946, the influential critic, Malcolm Cowley, assembled, and wrote a memorable introduction to, *The Portable*

Faulkner. Cowley, aided by Robert Penn Warren's glowing review and comments, convinced the reading world that Faulkner's work was immortal, worthy of comparison with the best literature of Western civilization. In 1950 Faulkner won the Nobel Prize and gained world recognition. When he died in 1962 he had, along with Warren, Thomas Wolfe, Eudora Welty, and others created the Southern Renaissance and permanently altered the direction, the tone, indeed the very nature of southern literature.

In the 1930s it was common to link Faulkner with the Georgia local-colorist, Erskine Caldwell. Critics coupled them as degenerate purveyors of sickening literature, "twin apostles of depravity, twin delineators of the benighted South."[45] Caldwell got the attention of readers—including scathing critics and millions upon millions of others—with *Tobacco Road* (1932) and *God's Little Acre* (1933), novels of degraded, sexually depraved poor whites. To the genteel, Caldwell was a pornographer shamelessly exploiting his subjects. He went on to write less sensational books such as *Trouble in July* (1936), about a community and a lynching, and a lighter work, *Georgia Boy* (1943).

In 1937 he set out to prove his critics wrong by showing that his characters were based on reality, that he had captured the real South. He teamed up with Margaret Bourke-White, the acclaimed and commercially successful photographer from the North, to create *You Have Seen Their Faces* (1937). By juxtaposing Caldwell's lean text and Bourke-White's stark photographs of a downtrodden people, the two produced a best seller. But it, too, offended many Southerners. The photographs could have been far worse, said Vanderbilt's Donald Davidson, who was thankful for "no candid camera shots of the harelipped girls tumbling lasciviously in the weeds. . . ."[46]

Faulkner was linked in many people's eye with Thomas Wolfe, who also burst onto the national scene in 1929 with *Look Homeward, Angel*, a sprawling, acclaimed autobiographical novel based on his youth in Asheville, North Carolina. Wolfe was not yet thirty in 1929 but he was obviously on the threshold of a dazzling career. He was a big, tall man bursting with inexhaustible energy. He wanted to cram everything into his autobiographical novels. He had moved to New York City to conquer the literary world, and in this he was acting as a romantic much like his major fictional characters—Eugene Gant and George Webber—whose quests would enchant several generations of critics and readers. In *Of Time and the River* (1935) and two posthumously published works, *The Web and the Rock* (1939) and his second-best novel, *You Can't Go Home Again* (1940), Wolfe caught the romantic, rhetorical South in immortal prose. Or so it seemed at the time. Wolfe's reputation has suffered greatly. He continues to have admirers, but to many today his novels seem sprawlingly verbose and undisciplined. He died at thirty-eight from tuberculosis of the brain.

African Americans added depth and sheen to the southern literary renascence. William Attaway's novel, *Blood on the Forge* (1941), celebrated the first great black migration from the South that started after 1910. This northward surge—a second great migration would start during World War II—caused lamentation among some whites who feared that the region's labor pool would be depleted. The irony of whites bewailing the departure of blacks was not lost on Attaway or writers like Arna Bontemps, Zora Neale Hurston, and Richard Wright. Bontemps' novel of 1943, *Black Thunder,* explored an aborted slave rebellion in 1800 and the white South's harsh response.

Hurston, born in 1901, grew up in an all-black town in Florida and did a variety of odd jobs before moving to New York City. She studied anthropology at Columbia University with Franz Boas, who assured her that Negro folklore was worth studying. She turned out stories and, traveling extensively, unearthed remnants of fascinating folklore, including music and voodoo rituals. By the mid-twenties she was a fresh face in the Harlem Renaissance. In 1935, after publishing in *Opportunity* and other black publications she compiled *Mules and Men*, a miscellany of folklore. Two years later she wrote her finest work, *Their Eyes Were Watching God* (1938), a lyrical dialect novel celebrating the variety and richness of black culture as experienced by Janie

Crawford, a strong black heroine. It is a powerful book, but few readers or critics—black or white—could then appreciate it, perhaps because it is a dialect novel and because it made no attempt to romanticize the earthy life of her subjects. Nor did she use the book to attack whites, who play a very small role in the novel. Richard Wright, writing in the Marxist magazine, *New Masses*, dismissed her book as a minstrel show and condemned it and the author for being "counter revolutionary." Alain Locke was both patronizing—he praised her knowledge of folk lore—and severely critical. When, he demanded to know, was Hurston going to grow up and write class-conscious fiction that provides a social commentary on race and racism?

A proud woman who was staking out new territory by showing that blacks could live full lives without reference to white culture, Hurston was wounded by the left-wing criticism of Locke and Wright. She wrote an angry, even "libelous portrait of Locke," says her biographer, but no one would publish it.[47]

In the 1970s, however, Hurston's novel was rediscovered and seen, as Henry Lewis Gates, Jr., has put it, as "a bold feminist novel, the first to be explicitly so in the Afro-American tradition."[48] The perceptive literary historian, Anne Goodwyn Jones, has shown that Hurston was one of many writers—Frances Newman, Ellen Glasgow, and others—whose work demonstrates that women were moving subtly and sometimes boldly beyond traditional assumptions about male power and the ownership of women's bodies.

Unlike the majority of black intellectuals, who had taken their stand with Du Bois's militancy, Hurston had from her youth revered Booker T. Washington's call for blacks to accommodate themselves to segregation and concentrate on economic advancement. And starting in the early 1940s, still smarting from the criticism from Wright and Locke, she became an avowed foe of Communism and of any left-leaning liberal who thought she ought to be a proletarian writer. Then in 1948 she was the victim of a completely false morals charge, which arose when a deeply disturbed young boy accused her of abusing him. She was finally and completely vindicated in the courts, but the trauma of the ordeal plus her advancing years and failure to please prominent northern liberal writers enraged and demoralized her. Bitterly angered by liberals, she attacked the Supreme Court's historic desegregation decision of 1954. Her views, puzzling to many who had known her earlier, her increasingly difficult personality, her bizarre behavior, and her fixation on writing about antiquity (of which she knew very little) left her isolated and penniless. Her last years were spent in obscurity. She would not live to see the great revival of interest in her earlier writing. She died lonely and forgotten in a Florida county welfare home in 1960.

Like Hurston, Richard Wright left the South—migrating from Memphis to Chicago—but his anger at Jim Crow and the culture of racism dominated his thought and directed his writings as he moved to the radical left and the Communist Party. He was haunted by memories of his youth in Mississippi and Tennessee; the sorry streets of Chicago added to the anger that overflowed in his writing and thinking. Born in 1908, he published his greatest work, *Native Son*, in 1940 at the young age of thirty-two. Wright's "native son"—he knew his title would infuriate much of white America—was "Bigger" Thomas who, like Faulkner's Joe Christmas, cannot shake off his violent anger and searing fear. "We black and they white," Bigger blurts out. "They got things and we ain't. They do things and we can't. It's just like living in jail. Half the time I feel like I'm on the outside of the world peeping in through a knot-hole in the fence." In a moment of panic the aimless young street tough murders a beautiful blonde woman who had tried, in a patronizing way, to befriend him. At his trial Bigger was defended by a Communist lawyer (this was Wright speaking) who made the clumsy argument that Bigger was nothing but a proletarian victim of a vicious class system. A bewildered Bigger was sentenced to death and died in the electric chair.

Five years later Wright wrote *Black Boy* (1945), a grim, barefisted account of his youth in the South. Anger burns his pages. As expected, Wright lashed out at lynchings and southern whites who had mistreated him (often brutally), but he also portrayed black culture as fatally stunted. The autobiography, like *Native Son*, immediately became a part of the decade's documentation of southern racism. The book was an immediate best-seller (while white southern critics heaped abuse on it) and Wright emerged as a major voice in American literature. But Wright, as it turns out, had bowed to editorial pressures to modify both *Black Boy* and *Native Son* to make them less threatening to readers. He toned down Bigger Thomas's rage and eliminated some extremely graphic and raw sexual passages involving him. Only recently, in 1991, did the original uncut version appear. Soon after submitting *Black Boy*, Wright had come to an agreement with his publisher and dropped the second half of his manuscript, detailing black oppression in Chicago. That section balanced to some extent Wright's denunciation of the South, but the deleted part, titled *American Hunger*, would not be published until 1977.

By 1945, with the publication of the scaled-down version of *Black Boy* and the end of World War II, Wright was the leading African American author and one of America's most influential writers. At this point he threw his hands up in disgust, quit the Communist Party, gave up on America, and moved to France. He never again recovered the magic of his early literary successes. Where had his creative genius gone? No one has answered that question. He wrote other books, but at his death in 1960 his great days were long behind him. He was fifty-two when he died in Paris, far from the Mississippi sharecropper's shack of his birth.

Their Eyes Were Watching God and *Black Boy* were important elements of the great wave of enthusiasm in the 1930s for documenting the depression South, particularly for documenting those who had been slapped hard by history. The New Deal's Farm Security Administration sent in some members of its top-flight photography group, including Walker Evans and others who produced a trove of remarkable photographs. Sometimes angry critics (including some historians today) have accused Evans and others of having their subjects pose in order to make their condition look as appalling as possible. The same charge was leveled at Bourke-White's photographs in *You Have Seen Their Faces* (1937).

In 1936 Walker Evans accompanied the writer James Agee to rural Alabama where they were to do a documentary article for *Fortune* magazine. For two weeks the two men lived with three wretchedly poor sharecropper families. But Evans's stark photographs and Agee's deeply sympathetic words offended the editors of a magazine designed to celebrate wealth and money making. The project was shelved. In time, after wrangling with editors and after Agee painstakingly rewrote his ever lengthening essay, a publisher was found for what was now a very long book, to be called *Cotton Tenants: Three Families.*

The book finally appeared in 1941 with the ambitious, biblical, but paradoxical title, *Let Us Now Praise Famous Men.* Famous men? True, the photographs were magnificent in their emotion and passion; even in his deceptively simple photograph of an old pair of worn boots Evans caught the pathos in his subjects' lives, seldom falling into sentimentality. More than Bourke-White, Evans breathed humanity into his subjects and influenced generations of documentary photographers.

Agee, all of thirty-two years old in 1941, felt humbled by the greatness of Evans's work. He told his readers that he, too, would strive with all his heart to be a camera with his words, but that Evans's genius and the wonderful humanity of the three desperately poor families—the Gudgers, Ricketts, and Woods—made him all too aware of his task and deficiencies as a writer. But he succeeded. In prose as dense and complex as anything Faulkner ever wrote—some of Agee's sentences run to several pages—Agee plunged himself and his reader into the moment-by-moment lives of the downtrodden survivors. His words leapt from his soul; he wrote in rapid, nonstop stream-of-consciousness style, with inner dialogue, candid, highly personal asides to the reader. Reverence pervades his words. Agee made his three obscure, dirt-poor families famous in the biblical sense of "Blessed are the poor, . . . the meek. . . ." Agee lashes himself. He taunts his readers: "by what right" do you observe these families? He wants to anger his readers and trouble their sleep. He makes lists of tattered, faded, dusty, worn-out articles: shoes, hats, dirty rag dolls, the oddments of small, shattered dreams. He quotes hymns; he rubs his hands in pain—not his own, but his subject's. He hints at incest; he confesses his own sexual longings. *Let Us Now Praise Famous Men* is a meditation on poverty, asking poignantly, why some are picked out for oppression and suffering. And hopelessness.

In places Agee's book is maddeningly self-indulgent and overstuffed. Sometimes his prose is out of control. The result: most of the critics hated it. One prominent reviewer complained that Agee was "arrogant, mannered, precious, gross" and cursed his book as "the choicest recent example of how to write self-inspired, self-conscious, and self-indulgent prose."[49] Commercially, the book was a complete flop.

Agee continued on, drinking and smoking too much and working to excess, like a failed romantic from a Faulkner or Wolfe novel. He wrote brilliant film reviews, a scattering of short stories, Hollywood film scripts (the *African Queen* was among his successes), and several novels. His greatest triumph came when his autobiographical novel, *A Death in the Family*, won the Pulitzer Prize in 1958. Set in Agee's hometown, Knoxville, Tennessee, the novel is southern to the bone in its story of family, place, tradition, and loss.

But Agee did not live to receive the coveted prize for fiction or to witness the rediscovery of *Let Us Now Praise Famous Men*. Like Hurston, Agee died before his lyrical cry from the heart about three obscure families was recognized for what it is—a masterpiece of intense, personal, passionately involved journalism. Agee died in 1955, the victim of an undisciplined life lived for art and love. He was forty-six.

There was a natural link between Agee and his contemporary, W. J. Cash. In 1941 Cash also published a unique, anguished, flowery, deeply southern book, suggestive of his yearnings to get to the bottom of things southern. *The Mind of the South* is a book written in blood, as Nietzsche would say. Cash's title is every bit as bold and controversial as Agee's. Both writers poured their hearts and souls into their writing, yet neither would live to see their books recognized as classics. Both men came from religious homes, though Cash, raised in a strict and theologically conservative Baptist church in North Carolina, soon lost any affection for southern religiosity while Agee remained a devout, mystical Christian. Like Agee's, Cash's style owes much to the grand rolling prose of the Elizabethan Bible. Like Faulkner and Wolfe, both men read widely in European literature, attempted to model their styles on Western masterpieces—Cash worshipped the novels of Joseph Conrad—and aspired to greatness. Like Agee, Cash had a fondness for drink, smoked too much, and always appeared to have slept in his clothes.

Cash early on yearned to be a writer. While a collegian at Wake Forest, he dreamed of writing an ambitious novel and talked about something he was given to calling "the mind of the South." He wrote for his college newspaper (as did Agee) and found it difficult to think of ever taking a "regular job" or having any sort of "profession." Both Cash and Agee suffered intensely in the process of having their books published. As early as 1929 Cash started publishing articles in Mencken's *American Mercury* that caught the eye of Alfred A. Knopf, who thought he saw larger possibilities for Cash's writing. But it would take Cash another dozen years to finish *The Mind of the South*. When published, it received positive reviews but modest sales. Driven to hallucinations by delirium tremens—alcohol withdrawal—Cash hanged himself in a Mexican hotel shortly after his book appeared.

The Mind of the South, however, has never been out of print, and few historians, even those today who roundly reject much that he argued, can resist quoting Cash. Like his idol, Mencken, who published his work and encouraged him to write and think big, Cash was fond of razor sharp contentions and personal, highly subjective verdicts. He meant to shock, to grab the readers' lapels and get their attention. His argument was complex and multilayered, but clear in its contention that there was one continuous southern mind. By "mind" Cash meant not what the region's intellectuals might be saying, but the ingrained ideals and the often unstated assumptions of the folk. In Cash's hand, the southern "mind" was a "fairly definite mental pattern, . . . a complex of established relationships and habits of thought." Southerners were products of the frontier; they were intensely individualistic, romantic, religious, violent, rhetorical, given to flights of fancy (and drink and fighting) in their hedonism, and, paradoxically, to deep feelings of guilt in their puritanism. To Cash, the South's "mind" was contradictory and ironic. For example, Southerners thumbed their noses at conformity but demanded that everyone think alike—particularly about religion, the sanctity of womanhood, and white supremacy. This demand for intellectual conformity, often enforced by the clenched fist of frowning public opinion, Cash called the "savage ideal."

He was, of course, thinking primarily about the white male South. Blacks received little attention in his pages, except as victims—of slavery, the white South's sexual lusts, political manipulation, and "Judge Lynch." Careless or unconvinced readers fail to notice that much of what Cash said about blacks he said about whites also. Cash attempted to sound the white voice and take his reader inside the "mind" he was delineating. Also, very few white historians of his time denounced slavery with his intensity or believed that lynchings and race riots occurred mainly because the "better sort," the social and economic power elite, subtly encouraged the white masses. Nor have many historians, even today, written as perceptively as Cash did about the psychological underpinnings of racism. Like Lillian Smith, Cash had read Freud and other founders of modernism in order to understand and to penetrate the psyche and ego (words Cash used with precision) of the white South down to 1941—and into the 1960s, before segregation came under intense attack from many quarters in the South and the nation.

The year 1941 was a turning point of sorts for southern writing, whether one accepts Cash's controversial, broad notion of "mind" or the view that historians should restrict themselves to discussing only specific individuals or groups, sometimes called elites. (The greatly admired C. Vann Woodward, whose interpretation of the major Populist leader of the 1890s, Tom Watson, appeared in 1938, has criticized Cash harshly for writing a book about mind while saying that in reality the region had no mind.)[50] But in the coming decades of change, many southern opponents of Jim Crow treasured Cash for his probing of the psychological foundations of racism. In a paradox or irony Cash would have loved, black as well as white Southerners in the Civil Rights Movement read him to understand what they were up against.

In 1941, William Alexander Percy, an eccentric Mississippi planter, poet, and lawyer, poured out his heart in his memoir, *Lanterns on the Levee*, another classic work of the Renaissance. Like his illustrious forefathers who had been Delta cotton nabobs for almost two hundred years, Will Percy was a racial paternalist and archconservative. He longed for yesterday's South—before honking automobiles and ringing telephones intruded and poor whites in their overalls got uppity, as they did in 1911 when they pushed his father, LeRoy Percy, aside in favor of the lowbrow, race-baiting James K. Vardaman in a bitterly contested U.S. Senate race. Percy's sentimentality and racism, however genteel, make for uncomfortable reading today. But for all that, his book is a haunting, beautifully written remembrance of things past. His nephew, Walker Percy, has creatively probed southern culture in serious, acclaimed novels from *The Moviegoer* in 1961 to *The Second Coming* in 1980.

By 1941 Southerners had bloodied H. L. Mencken's nose and knocked him down for the count. Together—black and white, male and female—Southerners had searched the soul of the South in memoirs, novels, histories, short stories, poems, and documentaries. The writings of Faulkner and Hurston, Cash and Lillian Smith, Agee and Tate, Wright and Woodward, and many others bring to mind a Dixie Special humming along the literary-intellectual railroad tracks with a speed and smoothness that take one's breath away. Native sons and daughters of the Southland had started to find their voice.

But were people listening? Not many read Hurston or Faulkner at first. Before the mid-1940s few Southerners had climbed aboard the Dixie Special and traveled to a new land. In 1936, Gerald W. Johnson wrote an article for the *Virginia Quarterly Review*, bemoaning the cultural life of the South. His editor suggested that he introduce Reconstruction and blame the Yankees' interference. No, wrote Johnson, "the basic trouble with the south is the social illiteracy of the so-called better element."[51] Cash agreed with his fellow Carolinian. Surveying the scene in 1940 as he put the finishing touches to *The Mind of the South*, Cash couldn't shake off a sense of futility, of tragedy. The South had intellectual leadership, he said, citing the Regionalists, the Agrarians, and the stars of the Renaissance, but many had been bitterly resented "on the ground that they had libeled and misrepresented the South with malicious intent." Cash concluded that the South now had "the best intellectual leadership it had ever had, the first which really deserved the adjective." But the great tragedy was "that this leadership was almost wholly unarticulated with the body of the South." A few were listening to this leadership, but the majority "were still affected by it only remotely and sporadically."[52]

Did it mean something rather chilling, Cash cried out, that the Southerner who had taken everyone's breath away was not Faulkner or any of his school of realists but Margaret Mitchell? Her book, *Gone With the Wind* (1936), at first seen as little more than "sentimental," had "ended by becoming a sort of confession of the Southern faith," Cash said dejectedly. In 1939, the residents of Atlanta and folks from miles around had lined up to see the grand opening of the film in a mood of religious ecstasy. "And later on, when the picture was shown in other towns of the South, attendance at the theaters took on the definite character of a patriotic act."[53]

But Cash and virtually everyone at the time failed to see that Mitchell was part of an overall attempt by women writers in the South—from Ellen Glasgow to Frances Newman—to find a gendered voice, one that moved beyond time-honored assumptions about a "nice" woman's supposed lack of real sexuality. In this attempt, Mitchell and other writers of the Renaissance were taking up what the Louisiana writer Kate Chopin had begun in *The Awakening* (1901). In Scarlett O'Hara, Anne Goodwyn Jones has written, Mitchell pitted "two types of female desire against one another, showing both Scarlett's erotic attention to the feminized Ashley Wilkes and her more stereotypical sexuality aroused by Rhett Butler's masculine force."[54]

But perhaps Cash, who was drawn by temperament to the tragic view, was too close to see that in time both his and Mitchell's work would become part of the Dixie Special that attracted more and more admiring passengers. If Cash and other despairing souls like Tate and William Alexander Percy were considered "wrong," perhaps it was because they sensed something deeply foreboding, even evil, in the future. Not so much in the future of their region, but in that of Western civilization and by extension the rest of the world. Cash, for one, worried himself sick about the rise of Adolf Hitler and the Nazis. Tate and his ultraconservative colleagues were under no illusion about the terrors Joseph Stalin would unleash in the Soviet Union. Before 1941 was over, the United States would be plunged into the bloodiest war in human history. The events and consequences of World War II were beyond anyone's power to imagine in 1941.

WHO SPEAKS FOR THE SOUTH?

After the slaughter and the glory of World War II—and, as usual, Southerners flocked to do their military duty—the South emerged in 1945 more prosperous and optimistic than at any time since the Civil War. The New Deal, with its infusion of federal money and programs that at least put a floor under the region's poor, had a significant economic impact. But the boom accompanying the war effort had a far greater and longer lasting influence. Military bases and defense industries pumped billions of dollars into Dixie and brought in men and women of differing views and skills. Cities grew faster than ever before. Parts of the agricultural South prospered greatly, but the rural South declined dramatically in population as several million blacks started a second migration northward, and pockets of rural poverty marred every state.

For intellectuals of all stripes, says Numan Bartley, the economic growth "the South experienced during the war and the social and political changes which resulted from it were the cause of the new positiveness in Southern writers and the South in general." But where, on the ever present question of race, would the South go? Would the white South look away, look away to Dixieland, or forward, to a genuinely New South? And how would the returning black soldiers, many of whom had seen and lived in a freer, far more racially integrated world in Europe, react to Jim Crow? They had resented the military's continued policy of keeping the races separated, pointing out the cruel irony of fighting against Fascism and Hitler's racism in segregated units. Charles S. Johnson, a sociologist at Fisk University, gauged the mood of his fellow blacks when he wrote that "the great majority of southern Negroes are becoming increasingly dissatisfied with the present pattern for race relations and want a change."[55]

And if blacks demanded a change—as they would start to do from the early 1940s on, and far more forcefully and unstintingly in the Civil Rights Movement from 1954 on—how would "the South" respond? In 1945 (and 1954) it was still possible in many quarters to assume that "the South" meant the dominant white culture. Were there enough emancipated whites ready to assault segregation? There were some here and there—Will Alexander, Sarah Payton Boyle, Ann Braden, Virginia and Clifford Durr, Lillian Smith, Aubry Williams—who were ready to abandon Jim Crow, but their numbers were few and the white leadership of the major interracial groups such as the SRC continued to assume that segregation was permanent.

Among politicians there were a few mavericks who were at least open to considering new racial departures, but the great majority were segregationists. "The very word liberal gradually disappeared from the southern political lexicon," Bartley has written, "except as a term of opprobrium."[56] The prevailing political mood found its voice in 1948 when several leading Southern Democrats, disgruntled at their party's emerging criticism of segregation and President Truman's civil rights proposals, bolted and formed the States' Rights Party. The "Dixiecrats," as the press dubbed them, nominated South Carolina's J. Strom Thurmond as its presidential candidate. But only four deep-South states went for the rebel ticket. Angered by the Supreme Court's monumental ruling against segregation in *Brown v. the Board of Education* in 1954, Thurmond and Senator Harry Byrd of Virginia pushed for a "Declaration of Constitutional Principles" and persuaded a sizable majority of southern congressmen to shake their fist at the Supreme Court and sign a "Southern Manifesto." Thurmond and Byrd led the way in a call for "massive resistance" to the Supreme Court's desegregation decision.

In time, the handful of moderate and liberal intellectuals found themselves operating against a backdrop of highly conservative public leaders who would move beyond Thurmond's comparatively mild racism and find expression in demagogues such as Alabama's George C. Wallace. In a historic speech in 1963 as he took the oath of office as governor, Wallace declared "Segregation now, segregation tomorrow, segregation forever."

That the South's all-male, all-white political leadership was stuck in the rhetoric of the past was obvious to the region's journalists, writers, professors, and preachers. And many of them, too, opposed abandoning segregation and allowing blacks to vote freely. But here and there were intellectuals and artists and ordinary folks who saw that a new day was dawning and that they must, as Faulkner said, "speak now against the day."

In the late 1940s and the 1950s the most liberal, some said radical, white voice for change belonged not to Faulkner—he would need some time to shift his views—but to Georgia's Lillian Smith. She had been a brave, lonely crusader against racism and Jim Crow since the 1930s. Born in 1897 in Jasper, Alabama, she moved in 1912 to north Georgia where her pious, Methodist parents opened a summer camp for girls. Smith's formal education was meager, but she was bright and she read everything in sight. She studied classical music for a while and then taught at a mission school in China before returning home in 1925. Somewhere along the way, Smith became what used to be called a "flaming liberal," particularly on questions of race and gender. Under her direction, the girls' camp and her home atop Old Screamer Mountain near Atlanta became the center of countless racially integrated meetings and conferences. She was the first white Southerner of any prominence to denounce not only racism and lynchings but segregation.

In 1936 Smith and her long-time companion, Paula Snelling, started a little magazine which in time became the *South Today*. The quarterly published articles by white and black liberals and moderates and became the springboard for many of Smith's ideas—such as her attack on the white South for being overly "protective" of women, partial to demagogues, a prisoner of tradition, and a repressive society haunted by ghosts of the past, fearful of new ideas and confused in its sexual attitude toward women and African Americans. Smith gained national attention in 1944 when her book, *Strange Fruit,* appeared. The novel is a melancholy tale of clandestine love between an educated, respected young white man of "good family" and a beautiful young black woman from across the tracks who, although college educated, works as a domestic servant. *Strange Fruit* was a "fantasy" about all human relations, Smith told her friends, but it was clearly a vehicle for her condemnation of sexism, religious hypocrisy, and racism and her acceptance of racial mixing—the taboo activity that the white South either vehemently denied (though it was clear that it occurred frequently) or blamed on black women as temptresses.

For a while the post office in Boston banned the book because of its theme of illicit love. Atlanta, still puffed up about *Gone With the Wind* (both the book and the film), read Smith's controversial novel but snubbed the author. (Smith had not endeared herself to her neighbors when she forcefully criticized Mitchell's book in a review.) Smith wanted readers to see that *Strange Fruit* was only incidentally about blacks and whites; it was about the human race and was a subtle probing of why societies condemn forbidden relationships. Given some of her remarks about the "real" meaning of the book, one has to think that she had in mind some justification of her own close relationship with Snelling at a time when homophobia was rampant and some of Smith's neighbors whispered about the two women.

Smith lived in a homophobic culture, but the South had no monopoly on that prejudice. Ugly rumors spread about her relationship with Snelling. Words like "odd" and "queer" were bandied about behind her back. She knew what people said. Their words cut to the bone. But it was one thing for an uncouth, bullying politician like Governor Eugene Talmadge to dismiss *Strange Fruit* as a "literary corncob." It was another to feel the butcher knife of abuse Hodding Carter wielded when he called her a "sex obsessed old maid."[57]

Smith was a genuine radical. She was uncompromising in her activities and pronouncements. When the newly formed SRC invited her to join in 1944 she refused. "We simply cannot turn away and refuse to look at what segregation is doing to the personality and character of every child, every grown up, white and colored, in the South today," she said. "Segregation is spiritual lynching. The lynched and the lynchers are our people."[58] She utterly rejected the long-standing conviction of the white South that it "knew" and "understood" the Negro. Like Cash, whom Smith published and reviewed favorably, she felt that the white South did not have any idea what blacks were thinking. But unlike Cash and, for example, Faulkner, who created some highly complex black characters, Smith made it her business to try to find out. From the 1930s through the 1950s she convened interracial gatherings, usually of black and white women, and for several summers in the 1940s she and Snelling traveled extensively through the South, listening and learning from the black community. She usually returned from such trips full of despair about the heart-wrenching effects of poverty and Jim Crow on African Americans but buoyed by their strength to endure.

In 1949 she dropped another racial bombshell with the publication of *Killers of the Dream*, a highly introspective Freudian autobiography. It too castigated what she considered the South's unholy trinity: white supremacy, worship of (white) women, and a fervid evangelical religion. Each corrupted the soul, she wrote, and emasculated the dream of decency and freedom. When the Civil Rights Movement shifted into social activism in 1955 with the Montgomery, Alabama, bus boycott, Smith embraced the crusade and remained a devoted admirer and friend of Martin Luther King, Jr. Following the Supreme Court's historic ruling in 1954, she announced in the *New York Times* that the *Brown* decision was "every child's Magna Charta." She then went straight to her desk and wrote *Now Is the Time*. Do the right thing, Smith proclaimed. Abandon the past and segregation! Look to the future. By this time Smith was battling cancer, but she remained an active advocate of civil rights until her death in 1965.

What accounts for Smith's liberation from the assumptions of her time? The answer is not simple or easy. Was it because she was raised in a deeply religious home; or because, at a tender age, she saw savage injustice in China? Or maybe, because of her sexual orientation and determination to think critically about southern women, she knew deep down what any oppressed "other"—including southern blacks—had to endure. Earlier historians might have "explained" Smith, arguing that women were tender and nurturing by nature. But what about the very conservative racial views of Margaret Mitchell and the anti-lynching advocate Jessie Daniel Ames (discussed in the next essay)? One might with profit point to Smith's deep immersion in the writings of Freud (also one of Cash's guides to understanding the South) as the explanation for her liberation from the social and intellectual restrictions of her youth.

At the other end of the spectrum of southern thought stood Richard M. Weaver, who ably, sometimes brilliantly, defended the traditional South. Born near Asheville in 1910, Weaver was a native Carolinian of the middle class who embraced liberalism, even socialism, during his collegiate days. But he changed dramatically, as he would one day explain in a classic essay, "Up From Liberalism." After arriving at Vanderbilt in 1932 to do graduate work under John Crowe Ransom, Weaver at first shied away from Agrarianism. Then he embraced it with both arms. He added historical depth to his faith in tradition and the Agrarians' suspicion of materialism and progress—Yankee sins—when he did a dissertation on the history and literature of the post–Civil War South, the era when the New South creed was being advanced with fervor.

Armed with academic credentials and a deepening distrust of modernity and everything connected with what he considered the Yankee mentality, Weaver left the region in 1944 to become a professor of English at the University of Chicago. Traditionally, it had been dissidents like Walter Hines Page who had left the South. But Weaver had seen most of his Agrarian idols, including Ransom, head for comfortable academic chairs in the North and he defended his decision to love Dixieland from afar, saying that "the sections fade out, and one looks for comrades wherever there are men of good will and understanding."[59] From his professorial perch in the city of broad shoulders, Weaver pondered the nature of the good society. He found it, not surprisingly, in the South of tradition, religion, family, and sense of place.

Professionally, Weaver made his name as a scholar of language and thought with acclaimed works like *Ideas Have Consequences* (1948) and *The Ethics of Rhetoric* (1953), books that on the surface have nothing to do with the South. But in his mind these books reflected his southern reverence for order and for universal truth, not social science "facts." He also pointed to masterpieces of art, to classical rhetoric, and to a social hierarchy that allows everyone to be comfortable by knowing their rightful "place" in society. From the mid-1950s on, as the traditional South found itself more and more on the defensive, Weaver became more polemical in defense of the South he had known as a young man. In various essays Weaver argued that the traditional South was to be prized for its hostility to hucksterism and money grubbing posing as progress and to an easily purchased skepticism masquerading as critical thought. Like his idols, Weaver would take his stand with an ordered, conservative, nonmaterialistic, and segregated society.

Like Donald Davidson—still at Vanderbilt guarding the gate against those whom he considered the vandals of change—Weaver looked with contempt on the historic *Brown* decision. Ending racial segregation would undermine everything good and decent about the South, Weaver believed. His voice now took on an edge. "It was not," Fred Hobson has written sympathetically but critically, that Weaver "ceased being a philosopher and became a polemicist . . . but rather that his voice assumed, if only to the slightest degree, the sharpness that characterized numerous other Southern voices during the late 1950s and inspired defenses of the Southern tradition that were in fact only defenses of segregation."[60] Weaver's attempt to outline a truly good society, while admirable in a general sense, was mortgaged, from first to last, to a profound lack of interest in and disregard for the feelings and aspirations of African Americans—or anyone, say, like Lillian Smith, who was out of step with the prevailing culture. When the former Agrarian, "Red" Warren, publicly reversed his earlier acceptance of Jim Crow and published *Segregation: The Inner Conflict in the South* (1956) and *The Legacy of the Civil War* (1961), saying it was time for segregation's funeral, Weaver blurted out to a friend: "Can you tell me what happened to Red Warren? I was dismayed by his *Legacy of the Civil War*. Some of the things I see there seemed to me incredible for a man of his background."[61]

A lifelong bachelor, Weaver died in 1963, alone in a hotel room in Chicago. His early death at fifty-three prevented him from assuming a visiting position—one that might have become permanent—at Vanderbilt. Nor did he live to see his dissertation finally published as *The Southern Tradition at Bay* (1968) and his name and work lionized by southern conservatives.

Lillian Smith was well known, sometimes in the sense of being notorious, and she helped the Civil Rights Movement as much as any white Southerner. Weaver, on the other hand, was barely known outside the groves of academe—and few readers of *Ideas Have Consequences* even knew its author was southern. Smith and Weaver are the last significant representatives of two dominant strains of thought among whites—the school of "guilt and shame" (Smith, Agee, and Cash among others) and the school of "remembrance" (Weaver, Ransom, Thomas Nelson Page, and their admirers). After Smith and Weaver's deaths, both schools continued to attract students. And if they were not of the stature of their illustrious predecessors they were still worthy disciples. Weaver's quest for a traditional, conservative, orderly society has been echoed by M. E. Bradford and George Core, writers and editors who have shepherded many of Weaver's writings to print, by the fourteen contributors to a symposium on *The Everlasting South* (1957), in the old-school historian Francis Butler Simkins's attempt to defend segregation as integral to *The Lasting South* (1963), and, more recently, by the transplanted Yankee-Marxist-turned-conservative, Eugene Genovese in *The Southern Tradition* (1994).

The guilt and shame driving Smith found a voice in Tennesseans Wilma Dykeman and James Stokely, who argued passionately in 1954, the year of the *Brown* decision, that the real South was *Neither Black Nor White*. They found in every state people of goodwill who were eager to bury Jim Crow. Among their heroes was Will Alexander, whose life they extolled in a felicitous biography, *Seeds of Southern Change* (1961). Like C. Vann Woodward, who argued urgently in the seminal work, *The Strange Career of Jim Crow* (1955), that there had been viable "alternatives" to the triumph of Jim Crow, and that nothing, not even segregation, was cast in marble, Dykeman and Stokely were in search of a "usable past," one that would show everyone that their South was not some monolithic racist culture. Their South was Arthur Raper, Agee, Odum, Smith, the CIC, Charles S. Johnson, Ralph McGill, and other independent voices. There were others, too: Alabama's Virginia Durr and her husband, the civil rights lawyer Clifford Durr; the Southern Regional Council's Pat Watters; and his colleague on the SRC, James McBride Dabbs, a South Carolinian who combined the running of a coastal plantation with civil rights activism, poetry writing, college teaching, and the penning of sensitive books.

As early as the 1940s, Dabbs, a devout Christian, began writing humane, cautious pieces on race for the liberal northern magazine, *Christian Century*. In 1958 he moved toward humanitarianism and probed *The Southern Heritage*, in an attempt to show that southern history held lessons for all who would take a stand against segregation. In this he was more temperate than Smith or Cash, thoughtful perhaps to the point of being tender minded and sentimental. Dabbs went on to write *Who Speaks for the South?* in 1964, arguing that God, in His infinite wisdom, had put blacks in the South to make white Southerners feel truly guilty, feel the weight of an immoral history, and see the moral path. Surely Dabbs's poignant words point to an unintended, unconscious assumption about human history—was God so concerned about whites and their salvation that He subjected blacks to years of misery? But no one who reads Dabbs carefully, or who studies his life and is aware of his deep piety, conscience, and attempts to persuade the white South to feel its racial guilt, would argue that he was a racist. Lastly, one must not overlook the reality, that Dabbs's piety and deep admiration for Martin Luther King, Jr., are at one with a deep, longstanding strain in southern religion of attributing the direction of human history to God.

Following in King's footsteps, Dabbs invoked God to come to the side of civil rights and to determine who should speak for the South. Dabbs, clearly speaking from within the tradition of guilt and shame, wrote eloquently on behalf of a South baptized in the moral waters of redemption through desegregation. He was, in a sense, the last in a long-standing tradition. By the 1970s such writing was losing much of its appeal. New books would be written in confidence, not guilt. "When the Sun Belt was wrapped around Dixie, the schools of shame and guilt and perhaps even remembrance," writes Fred Hobson, "were gone forever. Southern sons and daughters now wrote books entitled *The Good Old Boys* and *Southern Ladies and Gentlemen*—entertaining books, delightful books, but books focusing on the picturesque, on the South as cultural museum and oddities."[62]

But that day was yet to come. And neither Dabbs nor Smith nor Weaver—nor Woodward and John Hope Franklin who worked behind the scenes to help the NAACP prepare its case against the effects of southern racism for the *Brown* decision—truly represented the majority of Southerners, white or black. The two most "typical" southern thinkers of the era when the question "who speaks for the South?" coursed through the southern mind were identified with the Deep South—Ralph McGill and Martin Luther King, Jr., one white, one black, but both very southern. Both were talented and intelligent; both loved the common people, loved them despite their faults. Both were optimists by nature, and both were destined, one might almost say fated, to have most of their adult years shaped irrevocably by the Civil Rights Movement. One of the two would have greatness thrust upon him by his admiring black brothers and sisters and in time by a swelling number of whites nationwide. The other, McGill, would seek greatness in trying to convince his fellow white Southerners that King should be the one "who speaks for the South."

For three decades before his death in 1969, McGill was the most respected and widely read southern journalist of his day. He was born in 1898 in the hills of East Tennessee and taught by Vanderbilt's Edwin Mims that poetry and literature were almost as much fun as playing football. McGill went to the *Atlanta Constitution*—to "the city too busy to hate"—as a sportswriter after a period with the *Nashville Banner*. Mims's teaching bore fruit, and his student gradually switched to reporting on social conditions in depression-ravaged Georgia. His writing combined a lyrical sensitivity and deeply felt emotions with tough-mindedness and insight. His columns on Georgia scenes juxtaposed Shakespeare with the drawling wisdom coming from the tobacco-stained jaw of a tenant farmer. McGill was a sworn enemy of sham and pretense. By 1942 he was editor-in-chief of the *Atlanta Constitution*. He wrote a daily, signed front-page column that was syndicated through much of the South from the 1950s on. He championed patriotism, good manners, civility, education, responsible journalism, and portions of the New Deal, though he shook his head repeatedly at proposed federal anti-lynching laws and, through the early 1950s, at any legislation that would compel states to ensure fair employment practices. Still, he was an avowed Democrat and, says his biographer, "an unabashed admirer of Franklin D. Roosevelt."[63] He had nothing but contempt for demagogues like Louisiana's Huey Long or Georgia's Governor Herman ("Humman") Talmadge (son of Eugene Talmadge). McGill also loathed Communism, Fascism, the Klan, lynchings, and the poll tax. He disliked labor unions and their advocates, though he made an exception of Lucy Randolph Mason, the high-born Virginian who recruited union members. McGill had legions of admirers, perhaps because, as John Egerton has said, McGill was like most people—not perfect but striving to do and think the right thing.

Temperamentally, McGill was Lillian Smith's opposite. He hated injustice and said so, but he was comfortable with his region and its people. He was seldom guilty of self-righteousness and sought, wherever possible, to see both sides and be moderate in his judgments, particularly when it came to judging a whole society. As a young journalist in the 1930s McGill instinctively sided with moderates on regional issues and even criticized groups such as the Southern Conference on Human Welfare and the NAACP. Still, he urged blacks and whites to sit down together and reason out their problems (he was one of the founders of the SRC) as long as any discussion of ending segregation was off limits and radicals like Smith were balanced by moderate members. Unlike Odum and Virginius Dabney—who ironically and rather abruptly shifted to political and racial conservatism just after his editorials advocating the end of segregation on public streetcars and buses garnered a Pulitzer Prize in 1948—McGill did not quit the SRC when it came out for integration in 1951.

In Dabney and McGill's boyhood days racial segregation seemed normal, natural—to whites. During the first decades of his career McGill believed sincerely, as did many decent white Southerners, that blacks also favored Jim Crow. But unlike Smith, McGill and some others refused to believe their ears at first. In the early 1940s, W. T. Couch, liberal editor of the University of North Carolina Press solicited a book of essays to be called *What the Negro Wants*. But when Rayford Logan, the editor, and the contributors said they wanted an end to Jim Crow, Couch lectured them on what they "should" want. He printed the book in 1944 with a disclaimer in a publisher's introduction. Two years earlier, at a SRC conference in Durham, North Carolina, blacks had demanded an end to Jim Crow. McGill was genuinely puzzled. As someone who shared the long-standing attitude of white liberals that they "understood" African Americans, McGill was as flabbergasted as Couch. McGill was hardly alone in the white community; he needed some more time to see that an era had come to an end: that it was no longer possible, as it had been for over fifty years, for someone to be a "liberal" and also condone or defend racial segregation.

In the meantime as he sorted out his views, McGill lashed out at the Dixiecrats, but he Red-baited liberals like Smith, though for the most part he maintained a gentlemanly silence about her. In private he despised her, partially, one suspects, because of her personal life. In the 1940s, McGill also attacked Walter White of the NAACP. Given all this, it is hardly surprising that he was not emotionally ready for the *Brown* decision. But McGill's national patriotism and innate decency turned him around and he began admonishing his readers to obey the law of the land. Then when moderation began to melt away and otherwise admirable politicians signed the Southern Manifesto and white Citizens' Councils sprang up to subvert the Supreme Court's decision by any means, McGill moved to side with King. What McGill demonstrated "more than anything else," said the observer-historian Egerton, "was the capacity of white Southerners to change, to repudiate racism and rise up to the standard of justice and equality so courageously sought by their black fellow citizens in the freedom movement."[64] In this, McGill's transformation symbolizes the capacity to change displayed by other white journalists such as Mississippi's Hodding Carter and Arkansas's Harry Ashmore. In the 1950s ten newspapers and editors from eight southern states, many of them like Carter working in an atmosphere of extreme hostility and often danger, received the Pulitzer Prize, as did McGill and Ashmore.

McGill at least had the luxury of meditating and thinking out loud as he made his odyssey from "liberal segregationist"—of the SRC variety—to champion of integration and civil rights. But for blacks, every hour, every day was one of potential danger. The etiquette of Jim Crow dominated every area of life where the races intersected, and even a casual glance at a white person, particularly a woman, or the slightest failure to grin and shuffle at the appropriate moment, could bring swift, brutal reprisals. The case of young Emmett Till from Chicago proved this in 1955. Jim Crow's reign of terror was such that any black protest in the late 1940s—when lynchings again shamed the South—was so dangerous that few blacks dared speak out. One who did, and who paid the consequences, was John Henry McCray, a black writer, editor, and journalist of Columbia, South Carolina. A leader of the state's chapter of the NAACP and a political force—enough blacks voted to make some difference—and publisher of the state's only black newspaper, the weekly *Lighthouse and Informer*, McCray spoke his mind. "What has the South ever done for the Negro?" he asked rhetorically, and then answered, "Nothing they didn't have to do. Everything that has been done has been done by the Negro, or by the threat of Federal court action."[65] But McCray was not immune to danger. One of his utterances was a technical violation of state law; a vengeful judge sentenced him to sixty days on a chain gang. McCray survived the gruesome ordeal and returned to his newspaper more convinced than ever that his cause was just.

But Jim Crow could not reach behind closed doors. Racial restrictions could not muzzle dissent or silence college presidents like Benjamin Mays of Atlanta's Morehouse College or writers like Margaret Walker, who combined the professions of poet, professor, and novelist while teaching for decades at southern black colleges. Her major achievement, the novel *Jubilee* (1966), was a sort of black *Gone With the Wind*, told from a southern African American woman's perspective. Debate, some of it loud, some of it heated, went on in black churches, on campuses, or wherever blacks gathered away from white ears. So here and there the segregated race dissented in one way or another. In Montgomery, Alabama, for example, the iconoclastic Reverend Vernon Jones spoke his mind forcefully. At Atlanta University, W. E. B. Du Bois taught in an outspoken manner from 1934 to 1944. "For the vast majority of [blacks], a return to the old patterns of unchallenged white supremacy was out of the question. For them, the choice of equality had long since been made."[66]

The simmering of black anger led to a historic decision in Montgomery, Alabama, in 1955. Rosa Parks, secretary to the local NAACP chapter, refused to leave her seat and sit in the back of a city bus. When Rosa Parks sat down, the whole world stood up—or so sang out her legion of admirers. Her dignified and quiet refusal to abide by segregation any longer touched off a courageous bus boycott that would jump start the Civil Rights Movement. But who should lead it? Local leaders turned to Martin Luther King, Jr., who had just arrived in town to become pastor of a prominent Baptist church, the departed Vernon Johns's congregation. Just twenty-seven years of age, but well educated, highly articulate, and heir to a long line of forceful Baptist ministers, King agreed to lead the local crusade. His life would never be the same again. Neither would the South or, for that matter, the rest of the country. Even in places like South Africa and in many other corners of the world, "We Shall Overcome" became the anthem of freedom from oppression.

Who was Martin Luther King, Jr.? What were his ideas, his assumptions? And when and how were his thoughts formed? What can be said about the quality of his mind, his intellect, his facility with soaring words that became the imperishable rhetoric of the age? Fairly or unfairly, his name and the great movement are virtually synonymous. He was southern to the core, and that fact shaped the Civil Rights Movement from first to last.

"Dr. King" as the world soon came to know him, was born on January 15, 1929, in Atlanta, and named Michael after his father, the Rev. Michael King. The boy—"Mike" to his friends—was officially "M. L.", as his parents followed the tradition of many blacks who used only initials for their sons, hoping to circumvent the white South's habit of calling even elderly black men by their first name only. (They called their other son "A. D.") Later, M. L.'s father, inspired by church history and a sense of destiny, changed both his and his son's names to Martin Luther.

Young Martin King, as many in the movement would call him, came from a line of black preachers who were of the people but also above them and therefore able to lead. His mother's father, the Reverend Alfred Daniel Williams, had transformed the tiny Ebenezer Baptist Church in Atlanta into one of the most important black institutions in the city. Williams was not highly educated—he had taken a few courses in the religion department at Atlanta's Morehouse College—but he was a man of charismatic character and spirited personality who preached hard-charging, soul-saving messages. His sermons were emotional, evangelistic, from the heart.

Williams, like many of the city's blacks, was seared by the Atlanta race riot of 1906 when violent white mobs terrorized the black community for four days, wreaking death and destruction. (Margaret Mitchell, a young girl, had heard and admired her father's tough words and decision to guard his house with a rifle.) When Williams's fellow blacks responded by banding together to form a chapter of the NAACP, he was one of the founders. Later when the "city fathers," the white elite, tried to push through a bond issue with no provisions for the building of black public high schools, King's grandfather helped rally others, black and white, to defeat the proposal. In the 1920s, Atlanta built Booker T. Washington High School. It was the city's first secondary school for blacks.

Martin Luther King, Sr., was made of stern stuff and cut from the same cloth as his father-in-law. "Daddy King," as he would become known, was born into poverty but he pushed himself hard and paid his own expenses at Morehouse. When God "called" him to preach he threw himself into his work, adding to the glory of Ebenezer Baptist Church (he assumed the pastorate of the church after the death of his father-in-law) by moving it into new, grander quarters that it still inhabits today. A good Baptist, he thought church and state should be kept separate, and his sermons were of the old-fashioned, arm-waving kind, stressing personal salvation. But none of that kept him from being a strong Republican (the party of Abraham Lincoln), a charter member of the Atlanta Voters' League, and a fervid supporter of his alma mater. Publicly, he had no choice but to accept Jim Crow. But he never gave it his blessing and, on occasion, he lashed out at bullying sales clerks or the police. Once when a policeman called him "Boy," he snapped, "I'm a man."

Of course, Daddy King hoped that his two sons would follow in his steps and hear God's call. In their youth, neither son gave any indication of wanting to be a minister, though young M. L. was taken around to neighboring churches to sing hymns and spirituals to admiring audiences. Like his brother, who early on made clear that he was not bound for the pulpit, M. L. had an independent streak and entered Morehouse following his graduation at age fifteen from Booker T. Washington High, saying he wanted to be a doctor. He was a serious collegian, always dressed in a dapper manner, prompting his friends to nickname him "Tweed." He ended up majoring in sociology, thinking early on that the law might be interesting.

Did Tweed—the young Morehouse man who gladly followed President Mays's pride in the college's academic standards and code of conduct befitting future leaders—give any inkling that he was unusual, that he was bound for some great fame? Only slightly. He belonged to the campus NAACP chapter and an interracial group of white and black Atlanta collegians. Later he wrote, "The wholesome relations we had in this group convinced me that we have many white persons as allies, particularly among the younger generation."[67] This was a theme King would sound often in his later years. He had been ready, he admitted, to "resent the whole white race, but as I got to see more of white people, my resentment was softened and a spirit of cooperation took its place."[68] He was a good, though not excellent, student—he was quite young, remember—who learned much from

Walter Chivers, a sociologist who prided himself on being tough-minded about race and class. Chivers hammered at his students that while racism was the obvious evil of their time it was grounded in an economic system that would have to be challenged and overcome. Mike King had a number of experiences in summer jobs that confirmed his professor's warnings.

At Morehouse, King received a good education in what used to be called the "great books"—works by Plato, Aristotle, Augustine, and on through writers such as Hegel and Marx, about whom King was ambivalent at this time. In a demanding philosophy course, King read Henry David Thoreau on "Civil Disobedience" and later pronounced it his most important undergraduate reading. But it may be that the most important lesson King learned from Morehouse and its demanding professors and inspiring president was the bracing awareness that "nobody there was afraid."[69] Listening to the many voices of the Civil Rights Movement, one is struck over and over again with the statement that after several hundred years of fear, the fear was gone. For King, who would one day sing out with his followers that memorable line, "We are not afraid, we are not afraid today," the great haunting fear of white folks and racism began to loosen its hold during his college days.

During the summer before his senior year, King delighted his parents by announcing that he had heard the call to be a minister. Daddy King immediately swung into action. Before the young man could be ordained, though, he had to preach a sermon to the entire congregation. Was he ready? His words were enough to convince everyone that here was a worthy steward, ready to become co-pastor of Ebenezer Baptist Church. A beaming Daddy King laid his hands on his son and ordained him to preach the gospel.

But M. L. announced that he needed more education. His father, resigned to his son's determination to have his way, agreed and paid King's tuition to Crozer Theological Seminary in Chester, Pennsylvania, near Philadelphia. King made a wise decision. By the standards of the day, Crozer was both theologically and racially liberal. The school was integrated (though the town of Chester was racially segregated) and King's class was especially diverse, racially and ethnically. At Crozer, King had good teachers who introduced him to the theological ideas and philosophical principles that would undergird his thought for the rest of his life.

At Crozer, students were immersed in Gandhi's philosophy of nonviolence. King was entranced. He would not fully incorporate Gandhian principles into his conscious thought until he was called upon to lead the Montgomery bus boycott in 1955, but the fundamental assumptions of confronting the oppressors head on but by nonviolent means were in his mind from his first year at Crozer. King learned from Gandhi that oppression had to be answered—that the time for turning the other cheek was over, particularly when the oppressors gave no indication of abandoning their power and pride.

King's professors praised and analyzed the writings of Walter Rauschenbusch, a Baptist preacher and modernist theologian from the turn of the century whose books outlined a dynamic view of Christianity called the social gospel. In *Christianity and the Social Crisis* (1907) and *Christianizing the Social Order* (1912), books King had heard about at Morehouse, Rauschenbusch argued that personal salvation, or "religious individualism," overlooked the various ways in which evil was embedded in social institutions, in the very structure of society—in factories, laws, and organizations. Rauschenbusch pointed to the skewed distribution of wealth, the social inequality, the physical conditions many workers had to endure. In *Christianity and the Social Crisis* he argued that the church must add "its moral force to the social and economic forces making for a nobler organization of society. . . ." The social gospel would have Christians—clergy and laity—commit themselves to transforming society. This was heady stuff for a young black man from the South. King drank it in deeply. But could he swallow the entire message—that the social gospel would, in time, build the kingdom of God here on earth? King wanted to believe that, and bits and pieces of Rauschenbusch's idealism would cling to his mind the rest of his life and give his rhetoric a messianic tone. "It has been my conviction ever since reading Rauschenbusch," King wrote in *Stride Toward Freedom* (1958), "that any religion which professes to be concerned about the souls of men and is not concerned about the social and economic injustices that scar the soul is a spiritually moribund religion."[70]

Crozer also reintroduced King to Reinhold Niebuhr's stinging criticisms of the social gospel. Niebuhr, the reigning American theologian of King's era, had begun his ministry in Detroit imbued with the social gospel. But he had quickly come to see that evil was too entrenched in institutions and individuals to ever be eliminated completely. In one major book, article, and sermon after another, Niebuhr pounded away at pride, at self-regard, at self-interest, as the one irreducible fact of human nature. Niebuhr's modernist thought was sometimes called "neo-orthodoxy" because he rejected what he considered the uncritical, overly optimistic view of human nature held by Rauschenbusch and many other theologians. In his politics and commitment to ending racism and social inequality, Niebuhr began his career as a political liberal who in his earliest days found much to admire in revolution and Communism. In time, though, he came to see Marxism as just another form of Western civilization's illusions. Theologically, he rejected much that was called "liberal Christianity" because he thought it fatally underestimated self-interest, which he identified as another version of original sin.[71]

Niebuhr's books influenced King greatly, especially *Moral Man and Immoral Society* with its message that religious idealists were wrong to assume that the social order can be redeemed merely by curbing individual egoism, self-interest, or pride. Sermons on brotherly love were fine but idealists needed to understand how deeply self-regard was embedded in all classes, races, and nations. Like countless other theological students, King could not escape, even had he wanted to, Niebuhr's claim in *The Children of Light and the Children of Darkness* that unbridled idealists are foolish because they underestimate evil; while pessimistic "children of darkness," continually underestimate the power of love.

King knew by heart Niebuhr's oft-cited dictum that "man's capacity for justice makes democracy possible; but man's inclination to injustice makes democracy necessary."

Niebuhr's arguments would convince King that the social gospel, while vital, was simplistic (perhaps foolish) in its view of the social order and sentimental in its understanding of individuals. King came to see that the social gospel was too optimistic. Niebuhr's influence on King's understanding of Marx would be even more thoroughgoing. King read Marx deeply and critically and he would never completely escape Marx's insistence on class, although Niebuhr convinced King that Marxism was at bottom another manifestation of the foolish idealism of the children of light. King would never become a complete disciple of Niebuhr, but he later admitted, "While I still believed in man's potential for good, Niebuhr made me realize his potential for evil as well."[72]

At his graduation from Crozer in 1951—as class valedictorian—the foundations of King's thought were firmly in place. He was what Niebuhr would call a "tamed cynic," meaning that while he would sound the trumpet of the social gospel he was no foolish child of light, expecting the sweet music of sermons on love and charity to banish social injustice. Still young and idealistic, however, King believed that the forces of goodness needed to be encouraged at all times and that evil people, particularly those blind to their prejudices, needed to be led by a Christian faith infused with a commitment to change the heart and actions of those with power. More than Niebuhr, King was at heart an optimist, convinced that America needed moral leadership.

While Daddy King waited for his co-pastor, King went on for a doctorate at Boston University. His doctoral dissertation examined the transcendentalist idea of God in the theology of Paul Tillich and Henry Nelson Wieman. Far more traditional than Tillich, whose definition of God and much of religion as humanity's "ultimate concern" deeply bothered many Christians, King rejected Tillich and Wieman's conception in favor of what theologians call "personalism," a more traditional Baptist view of God. His thesis was hurriedly written while he was beginning his pastoral duties and during the first days of the Civil Rights Movement, and King received his doctorate in 1955.

King made ready to return to the South. He knew he would be preaching to folks who would value their minister more for his sincerity, disciplined, powerful pulpit oratory, and unshakable belief in God and in the equality of all Christians than for abstract theology or "Niebuhrian" ideas. His parishioners would approve of his beautiful, socially conscious wife, Coretta Scott King, from Alabama, who had been studying at the New England Conservatory of Music when King met her. She was as deep and multifaceted as the new Dr. King.

Together they returned, not to Ebenezer Baptist Church in Atlanta—Daddy King would just have to wait a while longer before his son joined him—but to Coretta King's native Alabama where Dr. King took up his duties as pastor of Montgomery's Dexter Avenue Baptist Church, where Vernon Johns had dazzled his parishioners. Unbeknownst to the Kings, the newlyweds were about to embark on a journey that would cause King and his allies, young and old, male and female, black and white, to shake the very foundations of America.

In April 1963 Dr. King was in Birmingham, Alabama. He was in jail for having broken the city's rigid segregationist laws. Denied even writing paper, King managed to pen a letter on the margins of a newspaper. He wrote to his fellow clergymen, and the letter soon became as famous around the world as "Bombingham" would become infamous wherever people thought about the events in America. King defended his Gandhian protest by citing Jesus, St. Augustine, Thomas Aquinas, Martin Buber, Niebuhr, the Old Testament prophets, Thomas Jefferson, and others, from James McBride Dabbs to Ralph McGill to Lillian Smith to T. S. Eliot. Here, certainly, was a clue to the cosmopolitanism, the internationalism of King's mind.

But a good argument could be made that King's ideas, those thoughts that propelled him to the front of the most important social movement of America in the twentieth century, were really homegrown, old-fashioned southern aspirations. Just weeks before he wrote his famous "Letter from Birmingham Jail," King drew up a pledge list that every member of his nonviolent crusade had to sign. It demanded, among other duties, daily meditations "on the teachings and life of Jesus," daily prayer, personal service and sacrifice for one's fellow man, refraining "from the violence of fist, tongue, or heart," and remembering to "walk and talk in the manner of love, for God is love."

If we forget for a moment that King was trying to give specific directions for social protest against what many called "the South," we see that his basic assumptions were the very beliefs that southern Christians—white and black, male and female—had at least been paying lip service to for almost two centuries. King knew that the white South of slavery and Jim Crow, lynchings, and often violent resistance to the Civil Rights Movement had not been true to its stated beliefs. His hope was that the South, and the nation, would come to share his dream of freedom.[73]

Since King's assassination in 1968 he has grown into a national icon. But like all icons he was also human, and perhaps in some ways a deeply flawed man. Recently critics have charged, sometimes with bitterness and disillusionment, that King's dissertation and many of his writings and speeches borrowed heavily from other writers. Some have accused King of plagiarism; others, including people who deeply admire his heroic role in the fight for civil rights, have argued that Boston University should revoke his doctoral degree. But King has his defenders, and the accusation of plagiarism, and its meaning, is still being contested.[74]

What is not debated, except by some extremists, is that King in his inspiring leadership, courageous actions, and finally his martyrdom helped bring about a South (and an America) where many voices could speak and not be afraid. Indeed, Martin Luther King, Jr., has become a world historical figure.

NOTES

1. C. Vann Woodward, "The Search for Southern Identity," in *The Burden of Southern History* (Baton Rouge: Louisiana State University Press, 1960), 14–17.

2. Henry L. Mencken, "The Sahara of the Bozart," in *Prejudices: Second Series* (New York: Knopf, 1920), 136.

3. Carl Becker, *The Heavenly City of the Eighteenth-Century Philosophers* (New Haven: Yale University Press, 1932), 15.

4. John T. Kneebone, *Southern Liberal Journalists and the Issue of Race, 1920–1944* (Chapel Hill: University of North Carolina Press, 1985), 33.

5. Bruce Clayton, *W. J. Cash: A Life* (Baton Rouge: Louisiana State University Press, 1991), 16.

6. Quoted in George B. Tindall, *The Emergence of the New South, 1913–1945* (Baton Rouge: Louisiana State University Press, 1967), 289.

7. Quoted in Fred Hobson, *Tell about the South: The Southern Rage to Explain* (Baton Rouge: Louisiana State University Press, 1983), 200.

8. Rayford Logan, *The Negro in American Life and Thought: The Nadir, 1877–1901* (New York: Dial Press, 1954).

9. Kneebone, *Southern Liberal Journalists*, 21.

10. Kneebone, *Southern Liberal Journalists*, 31.

11. Quoted in Clayton, *Cash*, 14.

12. Joel Williamson, *William Faulkner and Southern History* (New York: Oxford University Press, 1993), 159.

13. Richard Wright, *Black Boy* (New York: Harper & Brothers, 1945), 203.

14. George M. Marsden, *Fundamentalism and American Culture, 1879–1925* (New York: Oxford University Press, 1980), 103; Paul Conkin, *When All the Gods Trembled: Darwinism, Scopes, and American Intellectuals* (Lanham, Md.: Rowman & Littlefield, 1998), 49–78.

15. Marsden, *Fundamentalism*, 160–61; Willard B. Gatewood, Jr., *Preachers, Pedagogues and Politicians: The Evolution Controversy in North Carolina, 1920–27* (Chapel Hill: University of North Carolina Press, 1966), 43; Tindall, *Emergence*, 201–2.

16. Kenneth Bailey, *Southern White Protestantism in the Twentieth Century* (New York: Harper & Row, 1964), 45.

17. Hobson, *Tell about the South*, 183.

18. Quoted in Gatewood, *Preachers*, 43.

19. Willard B. Gatewood, Jr., "After Scopes: Evolution in the South," in *The South Is Another Land*, ed. Bruce Clayton and John A. Salmond (New York: Greenwood Press, 1987), 127.

20. Tindall, *Emergence*, 201.

21. Quoted in Tindall, *Emergence*, 203–4

22. Gatewood, *Preachers*, 13–26.

23. Quoted in Gatewood, *Preachers*, 30–31.

24. Quoted in Gatewood, *Preachers*, 44.

25. Gatewood, *Preachers*, 38, 43, 45–48.

26. For the best and most recent account of the Scopes Trial, see Edward J. Larson, *Summer for the Gods: The Scopes Trial and America's Continuing Debate over Science and Religion* (New York: Basic Books, 1997); see also Conkin, *When All the Gods Trembled*, 79–110.

27. Marsden, *Fundamentalism*, 190.

28. Quoted in Bailey, *Protestantism*, 61; Marsden, *Fundamentalism*, 190.

29. Edwin Mims, *The Advancing South: Stories of Progress and Reaction* (New York: Doubleday, Page, 1926), 296, 303.

30. Virginius Dabney, *Liberalism in the South* (Chapel Hill: University of North Carolina Press, 1932), 353; Kirkland is quoted in Mims, *Advancing South*, 157; Bryan is quoted in John M. Bradbury, *The Fugitives: A Critical Account* (Chapel Hill: University of North Carolina Press, 1958), 10–11.

31. Gatewood, *Preachers*, 128; W. J. Cash, *The Mind of the South* (New York: Knopf, 1941), 346–47.

32. Gatewood, "After Scopes," 128, 129.

33. Twelve Southerners, "Introduction," in *I'll Take My Stand: The South and the Agrarian Tradition*, ed. Louis D. Rubin (New York: Harper & Row, 1930, 1962), xix.

34. Paul Conkin, *The Southern Agrarians* (Knoxville: University of Tennessee Press, 1988), 85–86.

35. Joseph Blotner, *Robert Penn Warren* (New York: Random House, 1997), 105.

36. John Egerton, *Speak Now Against the Day: The Generation Before the Civil Rights Movement* (New York: Knopf, 1994), 65.

37. Cash, *Mind*, 393–94.

38. Egerton, *Speak Now*, 64–81.

39. Tindall, *Emergence*, 583.

40. Morton Sosna, *In Search of the Silent South: Liberals and the Race Issue* (New York: Columbia University Press, 1977), 42–59.

41. Quoted in Kneebone, *Southern Liberal Journalists*, 145.

42. Richard H. King, *A Southern Renaissance: The Cultural Awakening of the American South, 1930–1955* (New York: Oxford University Press, 1980), 48.

43. Quoted in Tindall, *Emergence*, 655.

44. Cleanth Brooks, "William Faulkner," in *The History of Southern Literature*, ed. Louis D. Rubin, Jr., Blyden Jackson, Rayburn S. Moore, Lewis P. Simpson, and Thomas Daniel Young (Baton Rouge: Louisiana State University Press, 1985), 338–39.

45. Quoted in Tindall, *Emergence*, 657.

46. Burl F. Noggle, "With Pen and Camera: In Quest of the American South in the 1930s," in *The South is Another Land*, ed. Clayton and Salmond, 191–92.

47. Robert E. Hemenway, *Zora Neale Hurston: A Literary Biography* (Urbana: University of Illinois Press, 1977), 241.

48. Henry Lewis Gates, Jr., "Afterword," in Zora Neale Hurston, *Their Eyes Were Watching God* (New York: Harper & Row, 1937, 1990), 187.

49. Quoted in John Hersey, "Introduction," in James Agee, *Let Us Now Praise Famous Men* (Boston: Houghton Mifflin, 1941, 1988), xxxi.

50. C. Vann Woodward, "The Elusive Mind of the South," in *American Counterpoint: Slavery and Racism in the North-South Dialogue* (New York: Oxford University Press, 1971), 261–83.

51. Quoted in Kneebone, *Southern Liberal Journalists*, 111.

52. Cash, *Mind*, 429.

53. Cash, *Mind*, 430–31.

54. Anne Goodwyn Jones, "The Works of Gender in the Southern Renaissance," in *Southern Writers and Their Worlds*, ed. Christopher Morris and Steven G. Reinhardt (College Station: Texas A & M University Press, 1996), 54.

55. Numan V. Bartley, *The New South 1945–1980: The Story of the South's Modernization* (Baton Rouge: Louisiana State University, 1995), 14.

56. Bartley, *The New South*, 71.

57. Quoted in Bruce Clayton, "Race, Gender, and Modernism: The Case of Lillian Smith," in *Varieties of Southern History: New Essays on a Region and Its People*, ed. Bruce Clayton and John A. Salmond (Westport, Conn.: Greenwood Press, 1996), 163.

58. Quoted in Clayton, "Race, Gender, and Modernism," 156–57.

59. Quoted in Hobson, *Tell About the South*, 323.

60. Hobson, *Tell About the South*, 330.

61. Quoted in Hobson, *Tell About the South*, 330.

62. Hobson, *Tell About the South*, 548.

63. Harold H. Martin, *Ralph McGill, Reporter* (Boston: Little, Brown, 1973), 40.

64. Egerton, *Speak Now*, 548.

65. Quoted in Egerton, *Speak Now*, 550.

66. Egerton, *Speak Now*, 553.

67. Quoted in David L. Lewis, *King: A Biography* (Urbana: University of Illinois Press, 1978), 24.

68. Quoted in Lewis, *King*, 24.

69. Quoted in Lewis, *King*, 21.

70. Martin Luther King, Jr., *Stride Toward Freedom: The Montgomery Story* (New York: Harper & Brothers, 1958), 73.

71. William R. Hutchison, *The Modernist Impulse in American Protestantism* (Cambridge, Mass.: Harvard University Press, 1976), 297–304.

72. King, *Stride*, 81.

73. Martin Luther King, Jr., *Why We Can't Wait* (New York: Mentor Books, 1963), 63–64.

74. For various views of this issue, see Theodore Pappas, *Plagiarism and the Culture War: The Writings of Martin Luther King, Jr., and Other Prominent Americans* (Tampa, Fla.: Hallberg, 1998), 65–84, 137–148.

Documents

1

"SAVING SOULS" BY GERALD W. JOHNSON (1924)

. . .   The tremendous effectiveness of these evangelistic operations in the hinterland is due, of
course, to the fact that they have relatively little competition. The
South and the Middle West are the two most fertile fields for
evangelists, and both sections are notoriously ill-provided with
decent public amusements. For the same reason the Ku Klux Klan
flourishes in the same regions. The drab monotony of existence
demands some relief. If the poverty and sparseness of the population make it impossible to support theatres and concert halls, and
if the communal *mores* prohibit horse-racing, cock-fighting and
dancing, the range of emotional outlets is sharply restricted. Evan-
gelism furnishes one—and that one is the public making of war
medicine. The evangelist, in the last analysis, is the eternal Medicine Man.

   . . . Certainly it is true that the evangelist's work tends toward
the suppression of such evils as spread syphilis and cirrhosis of the
liver, fractured skulls and involuntary bankruptcy. By providing
bored communities with a better show attended by less personal
danger, it tends also to discourage lynching. By exhausting the
honest workman's capacity for emotion of any sort it tends to
discourage strikes, as astute cotton manufacturers in the South
have discovered.

   . . . There are Christians who can forgive all else save the use
of the name of the Nazarene to preach hatred, bigotry and all
uncharitableness. Not a few of them are orthodox clergymen who

see in the goatish gambolings of the hedge-priests the destruction of their labor of years. But of one charge frequently brought against him the evangelist can be acquitted. He is not a hypocrite. Contrary to a somewhat widespread belief, Mr. Pecksniff cannot long put it over *hoi polloi* if *hoi polloi* can actually see and hear him. You can fool all of the people some of the time, and educated people, perhaps, all the time, but you cannot fool the riff-raff all the time.

. . . He is well paid—it is a poor evangelist who cannot pull down $500 a week while he is working—for no more distasteful labor than bullying his audiences and abusing people he dislikes; and in addition to the cash his work assures him a harp, a crown, and a mansion on high when his labors on earth are ended.

2

"ODE TO THE CONFEDERATE DEAD" BY ALLEN TATE (1926–1936)

Row after row with strict impunity
The headstones yield their names to the element,
The wind whirrs without recollection;
In the riven troughs the splayed leaves
Pile up, of nature the casual sacrament
To the seasonal eternity of death;
Then driven by the fierce scrutiny
Of heaven to their election in the vast breath,
They sough the rumor of mortality.

Autumn is desolation in the plot
Of a thousand acres where these memories grow
From the inexhaustible bodies that are not
Dead, but feed the grass row after rich row.
Think of the autumns that have come and gone!—
Ambitious November with the humors of the year,
With a particular zeal for every slab,
Staining the uncomfortable angels that rot
On the slabs, a wing chipped here, an arm there:
The brute curiosity of an angel's stare
Turns you, like them, to stone,
Transforms the heaving air
Till plunged to a heavier world below
You shift your sea-space blindly
Heaving, turning like the blind crab.

• • • •

We shall say only, the leaves whispering
In the improbable mist of nightfall
That flies on multiple wing:
Night is the beginning and the end
And in between the ends of distraction
Waits mute speculation, the patient curse
That stones the eyes, or like the jaguar leaps
For his own image in a jungle pool, his victim.

What shall we say who have knowledge
Carried to the heart? Shall we take the act
To the grave? Shall we, more hopeful, set up the grave
In the house? The ravenous grave?

                            Leave now
The shut gate and the decomposing wall:
The gentle serpent, green in the mulberry bush,
Riots with his tongue through the hush—
Sentinel of the gave who counts us all!

3

WILLIAM FAULKNER'S NOBEL PRIZE ACCEPTANCE SPEECH (DECEMBER 10, 1950)

I feel that this award was not made to me as a man, but to my work—a life's work in the agony and sweat of the human spirit, not for glory and least of all for profit, but to create out of the materials of the human spirit something which did not exist before. So this award is only mine in trust. It will not be difficult to find a dedication for the money part of it commensurate with the purpose and significance of its origin. But I would like to do the same with the acclaim too, by using this moment as a pinnacle from which I might be listened to by the young men and women already dedicated to the same anguish and travail, among whom is already that one who will some day stand where I am standing.

Our tragedy today is a general and universal physical fear so long sustained by now that we can even bear it. There are no longer problems of the spirit. There is only one question: When will I be blown up? Because of this, the young man or woman writing today has forgotten the problems of the human heart in conflict with itself which alone can make good writing because only that is worth writing about, worth the agony and the sweat.

He must learn them again. He must teach himself that the basest of all things is to be afraid: and, teaching himself that, forget it forever, leaving no room in his workshop for anything but the old verities and truths of the heart, the universal truths lacking which any story is ephemeral and doomed—love and honor and pity and pride and compassion and sacrifice. Until he does so, he labors under a curse. He writes not of love but of lust, of defeats in which nobody loses anything of value, of victories without hope and, worst of all, without pity or compassion. His griefs grieve on no universal bones, leaving no scars. He writes not of the heart but of the glands.

Until he learns these things, he will write as though he stood among and watched the end of man. I decline to accept the end of man. It is easy enough to say that man is immortal simply because he will endure: that when the last ding-dong of doom has clanged and faded from the last worthless rock hanging tideless in the last red and dying evening, that even then there will still be one more sound: that of his puny inexhaustible voice, still talking. I refuse to accept this. I believe that man will not merely endure: he will prevail. He is immortal, not because he alone among creatures has an inexhaustible voice, but because he has a soul, a spirit capable of compassion and sacrifice and endurance. The poet's, the writer's, duty is to write about these things. It is his privilege to help man endure by lifting his heart, by reminding him of the courage and honor and hope and pride and compassion and pity and sacrifice which have been the glory of his past. The poet's voice need not merely be the record of man, it can be one of the props, the pillars to help him endure and prevail.

4

LETTER FROM LILLIAN SMITH TO MARTIN LUTHER KING, JR. (MARCH 10, 1956)

March 10, 1956

Dear Dr. King:

I have with a profound sense of fellowship and admiration been watching your work in Montgomery. I cannot begin to tell you how effective it seems to me, although I must confess I have watched it only at long distance.

It is the right way. Only through persuasion, love, goodwill, and firm nonviolent resistance can the change take place in our South. Perhaps in a northern city this kind of nonviolent, persuasive resistance would either be totally misinterpreted or else find nothing in the whites which could be appealed to. But in our South, the whites, too, share the profoundly religious symbols you are using and respond to them on a deep level of their hearts and minds. Their imaginations are stirred: the waters are troubled.

You seem to be going at it in such a wise way. I want to come down as soon as I can and talk quietly with you about it. For I have nothing to go on except television reports and newspaper reports. But these have been surprisingly sympathetic to the 40,000 Negroes in Montgomery who are taking part in this resistance movement. But I have been in India twice; I followed the Gandhian movement long before it became popular in this country. I, myself, being a Deep South white, reared in a religious home and the Methodist church realize the deep ties of common songs, common prayer, common symbols that bind our two races together on a religio-mystical level, even as another brutally mythic idea, the concept of White Supremacy, tears our two people apart.

Ten years ago, I wrote Dr. Benjamin Mays in Atlanta suggesting that the Negroes begin a non-violent religious movement. But the time had not come for it, I suppose. Now it is here; now it has found you and others perhaps, too, in Montgomery who seem to be steering it wisely and well.

I want to help you with money just as soon as I can; I cannot, just now; I have had cancer for three years and have been unable to make much of a living during this time; also have found it an expensive illness. My home, also, was burned this winter by two young white boys; [. . .]. But I will have a turn of luck soon, I hope, and just as soon as I do I shall send your group some money.

In lieu of money, I send my encouragement and just a spoonful of advice: don't let outsiders come in and ruin your movement. This kind of thing has to be indigenous; it has to be kept within the boundaries of the local situation. You know the fury a northern accent arouses in the confused South—especially if that accent goes along with a white face. Keep the northern do-gooders out (sincere and honest as they may be); tell them to help you with their publicity in the North, giving you a sympathetic and honest press; tell them to send money if they are able to do so; tell them to try to use some of these methods in their northern communities. But don't, please, my friend, let them come down and ruin what you are doing so well. It will then seem to the country a "conspiracy" instead of a spontaneous religio-social movement. It has had a tremendous effect on the conscience of the people everywhere. But it won't have, if these people come in. . . .

5

MARTIN LUTHER KING, JR.'S LETTER FROM BIRMINGHAM CITY JAIL (APRIL 16, 1963)

My dear Fellow Clergymen,

While confined here in the Birmingham city jail, I came across your recent statement calling our present activities "unwise and untimely." Seldom, if ever, do I pause to answer criticism of my work and ideas. If I sought to answer all of the criticisms that cross my desk, my secretaries would be engaged in little else in the course of the day, and I would have no time for constructive work. But since I feel that you are men of genuine good will and your criticisms are sincerely set forth, I would like to answer your statement in what I hope will be patient and reasonable terms.

I think I should give the reason for my being in Birmingham, since you have been influenced by the argument of "outsiders coming in." I have the honor of serving as president of the Southern Christian Leadership Conference, an organization operating in every southern state, with headquarters in Atlanta, Georgia. . . .

I am in Birmingham because injustice is here. Just as the eighth century prophets left their little villages and carried their "thus saith the Lord" far beyond the boundaries of their hometowns; and just as the Apostle Paul left his little village of Tarsus and carried the gospel of Jesus Christ to practically every hamlet and city of the Graeco-Roman world, I too am compelled to carry the gospel of freedom beyond my particular hometown. Like Paul, I must constantly respond to the Macedonian call for aid.

Moreover, I am cognizant of the interrelatedness of all communities and states. I cannot sit idly by in Atlanta and not be concerned about what happens in Birmingham. Injustice anywhere is a threat to justice everywhere. We are caught in an inescapable network of mutuality, tied in a single garment of destiny. Whatever affects one directly affects all indirectly. Never again can we afford to live with the narrow, provincial "outside agitator" idea. Anyone who lives in the United States can never be considered an outsider anywhere in this country. . . .

Birmingham is probably the most thoroughly segregated city in the United States. Its ugly record of police brutality is known in every section of this country. Its injust treatment of Negroes in the courts is a notorious reality. There have been more unsolved bombings of Negro homes and churches in Birmingham than any city in this nation. These are the hard, brutal and unbelievable facts. On the basis of these conditions Negro leaders sought to negotiate with the city fathers. But the political leaders consistently refused to engage in good faith negotiation. . . .

You may well ask, "Why direct action? Why sit-ins, marches, etc.? Isn't negotiation a better path?" You are exactly right in your call for negotiation. Indeed, this is the purpose of direct action. Nonviolent direct action seeks to create such a crisis and establish such creative tension that a community that has constantly refused to negotiate is forced to confront the issue. It seeks so to dramatize the issue that it can no longer be ignored. I just referred to the creation of tension as a part of the work of the nonviolent resister. This may sound rather shocking. But I must confess that I am not afraid of the word tension. I have earnestly worked and preached against violent tension, but there is a type of constructive nonviolent tension that is necessary for growth. Just as Socrates felt that it was necessary to create a tension in the mind so that individuals could rise from the bondage of myths and half-truths to the unfettered realm of creative analysis and objective appraisal, we must see the need of having nonviolent gadflies to create the kind of tension in society that will help men to rise from the dark depths of prejudice and racism to the majestic heights of understanding and brotherhood. So the purpose of the direct action is to create a situation so crisis-packed that it will inevitably open the door to negotiation. We, therefore, concur with you in your call for negotiation. Too long has our beloved Southland been bogged down in the tragic attempt to live in monologue rather than dialogue. . . .

History is the long and tragic story of the fact that privileged groups seldom give up their privileges voluntarily. Individuals may see the moral light and voluntarily give up their unjust posture; but as Reinhold Niebuhr has reminded us, groups are more immoral than individuals.

We know through painful experience that freedom is never voluntarily given by the oppressor; it must be demanded by the oppressed. . . .

One may well ask, "How can you advocate breaking some laws and obeying others?" The answer is found in the fact that there are two types of laws: there are *just* and there are *unjust* laws. I would agree with Saint Augustine that "An unjust law is no law at all."

Now what is the difference between the two? How does one determine when a law is just or unjust? A just law is a man-made code that squares with the moral law or the law of God. An unjust law is a code that is out of harmony with the moral law. To put it in the terms of Saint Thomas Aquinas, an unjust law is a human law that is not rooted in eternal and natural law. Any law that uplifts human personality is just. Any law that degrades human personality is unjust. All segregation statutes are unjust because segregation distorts the soul and damages the personality. It gives the segregator a false sense of superiority, and the segregated a false sense of inferiority. To use the words of Martin Buber, the great Jewish philosopher, segregation substitutes an "I-it" relationship for the "I-thou" relationship, and ends up relegating persons to the status of things. So segregation is not only politically, economically and sociologically unsound, but it is morally wrong and sinful. Paul Tillich has said that sin is separation. Isn't segregation an existential expression of man's tragic separation, an expression of his awful estrangement, his terrible sinfulness? So I can urge men to disobey segregation ordinances because they are morally wrong. . . .

First, I must confess that over the last few years I have been gravely disappointed with the white moderate. I have almost reached the regrettable conclusion that the Negro's great stumbling block in the stride toward freedom is not the White Citizen's Counciler or the Ku Klux Klanner, but the white moderate who is more devoted to "order" than to justice; who prefers a negative peace which is the absence of tension to a positive peace which is the presence of justice; who constantly says, "I agree with you in the goal you seek, but I can't agree with your methods of direct action"; who paternalistically feels that he can set the timetable for another man's freedom; who lives by the myth of time and who constantly advised the Negro to wait until a "more convenient season." Shallow understanding from people of good will is more frustrating than absolute misunderstanding from people of ill will. Lukewarm acceptance is much more bewildering than outright rejection. . . .

I had hoped that the white moderate would understand that the present tension of the South is merely a necessary phase of the transition from an obnoxious negative peace, where the Negro passively accepted his unjust plight, to a substance-filled positive peace, where all men will respect the dignity and worth of human personality. . . .

But as I continued to think about the matter I gradually gained a bit of satisfaction from being considered an extremist. Was not Jesus an extremist in love—"Love your enemies, bless them that curse you, pray for them that despitefully use you." Was not Amos an extremist for justice—"Let justice roll down like waters and righteousness like a mighty stream." Was not Paul an extremist for the gospel of Jesus Christ—"I bear in my body the marks of the Lord Jesus." Was not Martin Luther an extremist—"Here I stand; I can do none other so help me God." Was not John Bunyan an extremist—"I will stay in jail to the end of my days before I make a butchery of my conscience." Was not

Abraham Lincoln an extremist—"This nation cannot survive half slave and half free." Was not Thomas Jefferson an extremist—"We hold these truths to be self-evident, that all men are created equal." So the question is not whether we will be extremist but what kind of extremist will we be. Will we be extremists for hate or will we be extremists for love? Will we be extremists for the preservation of injustice—or will we be extremists for the cause of justice? In that dramatic scene on Calvary's hill, three men were crucified. We must not forget that all three were crucified for the same crime—the crime of extremism. Two were extremists for immorality, and thusly fell below their environment. The other, Jesus Christ, was an extremist for love, truth and goodness, and thereby rose above his environment. So, after all, maybe the South, the nation and the world are in dire need of creative extremists. . . .

I have travelled the length and breadth of Alabama, Mississippi and all the other southern states. On sweltering summer days and crisp autumn mornings I have looked at her beautiful churches with their lofty spires pointing heavenward. I have beheld the impressive outlay of her massive religious education buildings. Over and over again I have found myself asking: "What kind of people worship here? Who is their God? Where were their voices when the lips of Governor Barnett dripped with words of interposition and nullification? Where were they when Governor Wallace gave the clarion call for defiance and hatred? Where were their voices of support when tired, bruised and weary Negro men and women decided to rise from the dark dungeons of complacency to the bright hills of creative protest?" . . .

I have no fear about the outcome of our struggle in Birmingham, even if our motives are presently misunderstood. We will reach the goal of freedom in Birmingham and all over the nation, because the goal of America is freedom. Abused and scorned though we may be, our destiny is tied up with the destiny of America. Before the Pilgrims landed at Plymouth we were here. Before the pen of Jefferson etched across the pages of history the majestic words of the Declaration of Independence, we were here. For more than two centuries our foreparents labored in this country without wages; they made cotton king; and they built the homes of their masters in the midst of brutal injustice and shameful humiliation—and yet out of a bottomless vitality they continued to thrive and develop. If the inexpressible cruelties of slavery could not stop us, the opposition we now face will surely fail. We will win our freedom because the sacred heritage of our nation and the eternal will of God are embodied in our echoing demands. . . .

One day the South will recognize its real heroes. They will be the James Merediths, courageously and with a majestic sense of purpose facing jeering and hostile mobs and the agonizing loneliness that characterizes the life of the pioneer. They will be old, oppressed, battered Negro women, symbolized in a seventy-two-year-old woman of Montgomery, Alabama, who rose up with a sense of dignity and with her people decided not to ride the segregated buses, and responded to one who inquired about her tiredness with ungrammatical profundity: "My feet is tired, but my soul is rested." They will be the young high school and college students, young ministers of the gospel and a host of their elders courageously and nonviolently sitting-in at lunch counters and willingly going to jail for conscience's sake. One day the South will know that when these disinherited children of God sat down at lunch counters they were in reality standing up for the best in the American dream and the most sacred values in our Judeo-Christian heritage, and thusly, carrying our whole nation back to those great wells of democracy which were dug deep by the Founding Fathers in the formulation of the Constitution and the Declaration of Independence. . . .

> Yours for the cause of Peace and Brotherhood,
> Martin Luther King, Jr.

THE SOUTH IN THE
DEPRESSION DECADES

John Salmond

By 1914, all the lineaments of the New South were firmly in place. "Progress," as W. J. Cash called it, and in particular the cotton mills, had rescued the "great body of the white tenants and sharecroppers from their estate as such," painfully transforming them into millhands, working and living in the hundreds of mill villages that dotted the landscape of the southern Piedmont. "Textile mills built the New South," observed Jacquelyn Hall, Robert Korstad, and James Leloudis. These same mills eventually destroyed the textile industry in New England, as manufacturers moved where capital was cheaper, and labor likewise—as well as plentiful and unorganized.[1]

Cash commented that "progress" also relieved the region's whites from having to work side by side, and on practically the same terms, with the black man, for few African Americans were permitted in the mills. Though hundreds of thousands of whites remained on the land, and large numbers of blacks moved to the growing cities and towns, Cash's observation remains broadly true. Southern whites and blacks lived apart, rigidly segregated in a manner that would have been considered ludicrous had it been proposed in, say, 1844. Moreover, segregation was enforced with a savagery that was also new, partly a product of the racist rhetoric that had accompanied the successful drive to overturn the outcome of the Civil War, to frustrate the intent of the Fourteenth and Fifteenth Amendments, and to remove African Americans from political life.[2] Having done that, it was then a relatively simple matter to circumscribe them so completely as to create a distinctively southern caste system. At times this system needed to be reinforced—hence the dramatic rise of racially motivated acts of violence that occurred from about 1890, but in general the ever-present threat was sufficient. By 1914, the South was emphatically a "white man's country," and though the Progressive reform impulse currently active in other parts of the country did touch the region, its southern advocates were forced to work within the confines of racial separation, effectively masking the class-based inequalities of evolving mill village culture. Despite some Progressive tendencies, "the politics of the South in 1914 was fully barred away from—as devoid of—social and economic focus as it had ever been in the past."[3]

American involvement in World War I did not change this fundamental structure, though it did create some strains within it. For the textile manufacturers and their workers, the war years were good times. The domestic demand for cotton cloth at home and abroad soared, more mills were built, existing mills operated around the clock, the increased demand for labor pulled more white families off the land, and, most important of all, wage rates tripled between 1915 and 1920. This meant that the economic rewards of mill work far outstripped those of the farm. Textile workers had glimpses of the good life, and they would fight to preserve them.

Southern blacks, too, seized the opportunities the Great War gave them. The main one was the chance to leave. Higher rates of pay in the northern factories greatly reduced the pool of available unskilled and domestic labor, a pool no longer replaceable by immigrants from Europe. Before long, northern employment agents were venturing South, where they found willing recruits. The brutalities of segregation, the ravages of the boll weevil, and the disastrous floods of 1915 and 1916 combined to mark the beginning of the Great Migration, the movement of southern blacks to the cities of the North and Mid West, the greatest internal movement of peoples in American history. Moreover, some southern blacks moved even further than New York and Chicago. They went to Europe, especially to France, as soldiers, where their welcome as liberators deeply disturbed the American high command, who feared that the experience would make them unwilling to accept their continued second-class status at home—as indeed was the case. Southerners were particularly bothered by this, though they were not alone. Rumors of returning blacks "who had been French-woman ruined" swept southern communities in the weeks following the 1918 armistice and provided ready fuel for the region's racist demagogues; 1919 was a year of ferocious racial violence. Blacks and whites fought pitched battles in the streets of Chicago, Charleston, and Omaha, while throughout the South lynch mobs gathered to reassert white supremacy. In Phillips County, Arkansas, the hysteria resulted in the massacre of more than a hundred rural blacks, and the intervention of federal troops. In Ocoee, Florida, an attempt by blacks to vote provoked savage responses. Whites blamed "impudent negroes," often returned veterans, for provoking the violence, and perhaps they did. If so, such riots can be seen as the opening salvos of their long war against the injustice of the southern caste system.[4]

Southern whites, too, violently protested the New South industrial order in the years following the armistice, again the first shots of a long and bitter campaign. The battleground was the textile mills, textiles being a "white" industry, employing only a few blacks, mainly for janitorial tasks. The spark was the sudden breaking of the textile boom in 1920. The decrease in demand for textiles following the war was the main reason, but there were other factors, including President Harding's restrictive tariff policies, which cost the industry lucrative foreign markets, and the dramatic development of the textile industry in South Asia. Furthermore, the vagaries of fashion affected demand for textiles. Shorter skirts meant less fabric per garment, while "showing a leg" also put an end to cotton stockings. The cotton industry quickly moved from boom to decline, and it never really recovered.

Predictably, manufacturers responded by cutting costs, and, in particular, attacked the wage gains of the war years. To their surprise, their operatives fought back, partly to protect the better lives they had briefly experienced but also as a reflection of changes in the mills' labor force. Family labor had declined and an increasing number of the operatives were now adult workers, men and women dependent on their weekly wage for sustenance. This was the first generation of workers to see their mill jobs as permanent, not just as a supplement to the farm. For the first time, workers considered organization as a means of protecting their lives.

From 1919 to 1921 industrial strife rocked the textile Piedmont, usually under the aegis of recently chartered locals of the United Textile Workers, an A. F. of L. affiliate, which for the first time made inroads into the staunchly anti-union industry, especially in North Carolina. Workers, determined to preserve their wartime gains, joined the union at such a rate that the UTW's central office could neither keep up with the demand nor provide inexperienced local officers with counsel or money. Though manufacturers were severely shaken by the disorder, they need not have bothered. Overproduction and the postwar slump proved a short-term boon for them. With plenty of replacement labor available, huge stockpiles of fabric in their warehouses, and the support of state law enforcement authorities, they were far better placed to deal with industrial strife than the inexperienced, cash-strapped locals. In 1921 North Carolina unionists forced regional strike action on reluctant national UTW officers. Mill management simply waited out the strike, and with its collapse, this first challenge to the New South power structure ended.

Textile operatives were not the only southern workers to turn to unions and strike action as the postwar economic downturn began to erode wartime gains. Oil workers in Texas and Louisiana found their wages cut, and formed unions as a means of forcing redress. Tobacco workers joined the Tobacco Workers International Union, giving it a southern presence for the first time, winning temporary wage increases for its members. Alabama mine workers flocked to the United Mine Workers' banner in 1917, in a strike that gained a substantial wage increase for its mainly black participants. A second, statewide walkout in 1920 was less successful. The owners fought back bitterly, there was violence, black workers lost their livelihoods or their homes, and the UMW was run out of Alabama. Black lumber workers who had joined AFL affiliates were also the victims of vigilante violence, particularly in Louisiana. If the union activity of 1919 to 1921 marks the first substantial attempt by organized labor to challenge the New South economic and social order, it has to be said that in every instance the power structure proved far too strong.

Yet, as George Tindall aptly remarked, "a subterranean turbulence simmered in the mill villages of the Piedmont" throughout the 1920s, even as industrial peace returned to the region. Textile manufacturers drew two conclusions from the postwar disturbances, conclusions also drawn by management in other southern industries. The first involved an abiding hatred of unions, and a determination to prevent their future formation in the South. The second was that simply to slash wages as a means of cutting costs was too confrontational: other means of achieving this had to be found.[5]

Throughout the 1920s, manufacturers restructured their industry, consolidated their holdings, modernized their machinery, and changed their work practices. Hard times and bankruptcies provided opportunities for men like J. Spencer Love of Burlington Industries to take over locally owned mills in the process of creating huge textile empires. They introduced economies of scale, brought in newer, less labor-intensive machines, and insisted that their workers work harder and faster, perform more tasks, and run more looms. They were able to do this because of a general labor surplus. Moreover, the mill labor force was changing. Women had always been part of it, because of the original family hiring practices. By the mid-1920s, however, they were much more likely to be hired as individuals, young, single women for whom mill work had become a normal vocation, and married women who needed the money and usually staffed the night shift, caring for their families during the day. Women workers often found themselves the victims of job reorganization, losing income as piecework rates replaced wages. Moreover, they no less than men always worked with the cloud of job insecurity hanging over them. It is scarcely surprising, therefore, that women were actively involved in subsequent challenges to the system.

The next challenge occurred at the end of the decade, when workers throughout the Piedmont again rose up against the changed nature of their employment: against the "stretchout," the collective name they gave to the new management practices under which they worked. In 1927, workers in Henderson, North Carolina, staged "a preview of the drama to follow," when they walked out in protest against wage cuts. Union organizers arrived, so did the state militia, management retaliated by evicting strike leaders from the mill village, and the protest ended as it had begun, spontaneously. UTW organizers, however, used the opportunity to move back into the South, and by the end of 1928 they had established locals throughout the Piedmont.[6]

Management and unions alike, however, were unprepared for the level of industrial unrest that swept the textile South in 1929. In that year, "despite the labor surplus, the power of management, the intimidation of union members," and the weakness of the UTW and other national labor unions, thousands of textile workers resisted the "stretchout" by walking off the job. The wave of unrest started on March 12 in Elizabethton in Tennessee, where the entire workforce of the Bemberg and Glanzstoff rayon plant, led by the young women of the inspection department, struck spontaneously. The trigger was the demotion of one of their number who had sought a wage increase, but the "stretchout" was the root cause. There was some violence (though no fatalities) in Elizabethton, especially upon the arrival of UTW representatives anxious to capitalize on events not of their making. The state militia was there to confront them, and so were various vigilante groups. The strike ended in May, with management the victor; its close connection with state power in Tennessee ensured this, as was to be the case elsewhere.[7]

The UTW became involved belatedly in the Elizabethton strike. In Marion, North Carolina, scene of the year's worst violence, the local UTW branch provided the leadership for a strike that lasted for much of the year. It involved a vigorous counterattack by mill management and local law enforcement officers, culminating in the killing on October 2 of six strikers and the wounding of twenty-five others, most of them shot in the back as they fled the picket line. Local union officials were jailed as a result of this incident, but the deputies who did the shooting were all acquitted.

Most of the challenges of 1929, however, did not result from union activity. In Pineville, in Leaksville, in Belmont, in Bessemer City, in Pelzer, in Woodruff, in Greenville, in scores of mill towns across the Carolinas, men and women struck spontaneously, having reached the limits of their endurance. "No," said a Greenville, South Carolina, striker, "we don't want no organizers from outside. . . . We're doing this ourselves." As a result, they too were bound to fail. The forces arrayed against them were too strong. Yet, by their action, they also challenged the southern power structure.[8]

The most famous single challenge of 1929, however, was union-led, but not by the UTW. In Gastonia, North Carolina, the industrial arm of the Communist Party, the National Textile Workers Union, organized a local at one of the South's largest plants, the Rhode Island–owned Loray Mill. There had been trouble there for years over management's "stretchout" policies, and in April 1929 the NTWU local, assisted by organizers sent from New York, most of whom were young, activist, "Red" women, called the workers out. Thus began a sequence of events which eventually gained national attention. Before the year was out the town's police chief, Orville Aderholt, had been shot, allegedly in a gun battle with strike leaders, and Ella May, a local mill worker and union activist, had also been killed, almost certainly by a member of a vigilante squad organized and armed by Loray Mill management. Governor O. Max Gardner had dispatched National Guard units to keep order at the mill, and eventually sixteen strike leaders, including three women, were put on trial for conspiring to murder Aderholt, in the largest group trial for a capital crime in American history. The eventual conviction of several of the accused for lesser offences, the involvement of the Communist Party in their defense, their release on bail, and the eventual disappearance of seven of them into the vastness of the Soviet Union has ensured that the events of the Gastonia strike in 1929 remain part of the mythology of the American left.

The focus on the "Gastonia Reds" tended to divert attention from the rank and file whom they led. These were no different from the mill workers of Elizabethton, or Marion, or Greenville. Women formed the core of the local strike committee, and were the activists on the picket line. Some were young women, who saw their futures in the mills and wanted more out of the modern world than their wages allowed, others were married women like Ella May, often women whose husbands had deserted them, or drifted away semipermanently, women who were determined to make a better life for their families. The fact that Communists led their challenge and prompted their particular activism does not make their purpose any less important. And, of course, they lost, as did their fellow strikers throughout the South. The murderers of Ella May went unpunished, though most people in Gastonia knew who they were.

It was not only the southern textile workers who challenged the power structure as the boom years gave way to economic collapse. Workers in the coal-mining village of Wilder, Tennessee, who had secretly organized a United Mine Workers local, decided to take on the Fentress Coke and Coal Company in 1932 after their wages had been slashed by 20 percent. In the long struggle that followed, the familiar pattern of the mill towns was reproduced: acts of violence, the formation of vigilante groups under management aegis, the eviction of strikers from company houses, the arrival of state troops, the murder of Barney Graham, the strike leader, and the eventual breaking of the strike. Like the textile workers, mine workers simply did not have the power to alter the condition of their lives through direct action. The forces arrayed against them were far too strong.

A year later, textile workers thought this imbalance had been altered decisively in their favor. As Bryant Simon has written, in "Greenwood, South Carolina, mill workers huddled around their radios on 16 July 1933." When they heard the news that the new president, Franklin D. Roosevelt, had approved the Cotton Textile Code of the National Recovery Act, the centerpiece of the New Deal plan to spark economic recovery through industry-wide controls on production, they took to the streets, singing, square dancing, celebrating what they believed to be a great victory. The code, after all, contained provisions for higher wages, shorter hours, and above all an end to the "stretchout." Equally important, it contained section 7(a), which gave workers the right to join unions of their choice, without employer interference. "The President wants you to join a union," became the slogan. Southern textile workers believed this; within the year, membership of UTW locals had mushroomed from a few thousand to around half the workforce.[9]

It was soon clear, however, that manufacturers had no intention of observing the Textile Code's provisions on labor. All codes, after all, were in the end voluntary; despite all the rhetoric about government-employer-worker partnership, the bodies responsible for their administration remained firmly in the hands of the employers. Reports came from all over the country of intensified stretchouts, shortened work weeks, reduced wages, and discrimination against union activists. Manufacturers, with huge stockpiles of unsold goods, had little need to keep up production levels; they used those code provisions that served their interests and ignored those that did not. All over the country the anger of the workers intensified, as did their determination to use the unions to force compliance. The national UTW leadership, though well aware of its financial and organizational deficiencies, could not afford to ignore the anger welling up from below. Instead, it tried to harness this anger nationally, by calling what remains the largest single-industry strike in American history, the general textile strike of September 1934.

Though the strike was national in dimension, those historians who have discussed it at all have tended to focus on the South, for good reason. The Piedmont after all, with about 70 percent of the nation's spindles, was the epicenter of the cotton textile industry and would thus determine the outcome of the strike. Initially, management was taken by surprise by the extent of support for the challenge and the vehemence and intensity of the workers, both women and men. Observers again commented, as they had done in 1929, on the presence of young women on the picket lines and as members of the "flying squadrons" of motorized pickets, speeding from mill to mill, bringing out the workers.

Nevertheless, the power remained with the manufacturers. The strike was called off after three weeks on terms that, no matter the spin the UTW put on them, represented a crushing defeat for the workers. There were many reasons for the failure of the strike, including the weakness and lack of preparedness of the union's national leadership, the ability of manufacturers simply to sit it out, and the determination of the president not to become actively involved. But at the local level, and especially in the South, it was the familiar combination of management and state power that ended this challenge, as it had ended those of 1921 and 1929. In the Carolinas and Georgia the National Guard was used to protect the mills, to curb picketing, and to ensure that manufacturers could continue to run their looms if they wanted to. Governor Eugene Talmadge of Georgia even imprisoned strikers in a hastily constructed "concentration camp," while in Honea Path, South Carolina, Trion and Arragon, Georgia, and Belmont, North Carolina, battles between specially sworn deputies and pickets ended with twelve strikers dead. Even as the New Deal sought national answers to America's economic collapse, in the South the region's power elite survived yet another challenge.

Mill management took bitter reprisals. Hundreds of strikers were blacklisted, denied mill work forever, despite the provisions of the strike settlement. Thousands more were reemployed only on condition that they abjured further union activity. The UTW lost its brief influence amongst textile workers. When union organizers returned to the South, they did so under the aegis of the lusty young CIO. The launching of the CIO in 1935 brought a new player into America's labor world, one determined to organize the unorganized and unskilled, the vast industrial workforce of America. The CIO also had a national commitment to organizing black workers in the same unions as whites. Though the thrust of its initial activities lay in the industrial heartland, CIO leaders nevertheless recognized that without a southern presence they could scarcely claim national standing, and that the key southern industry was textiles. They also knew that organizing textiles was going to be a long, fierce struggle, but at least the race question was not paramount, for it was a white industry. Accordingly the CIO decided that its first southern campaign should be in the mills and from 1937 began to wage it, under the control of Sidney Hillman and the Textile Workers Organizing Committee (TWOC). The battle was indeed hard: the ferocious combination of state and mill power, the fear among the workers, and the general regional hostility to militant unionism meant that progress was fearfully slow. After two years, for all their effort, TWOC organizers had signed up only 2 percent of the textile workers. The memory of the 1934 defeat was too recent in workers' minds—including the promises of relief that never came, their powerlessness when the strike was ended, and the hollowness of the so-called "victory" UTW leaders had announced. The drive ended in May 1939, but the Textile Workers Union of America (TWUA-CIO), which replaced the TWOC, contained some southern locals, usually survivors of 1934, providing a modest platform for future challenges.

Moreover, other CIO unions had begun work in the South, usually on their own initiative, and determined to work on a biracial basis. "In the tobacco factories of North Carolina and the iron mines and smelters of Alabama, these organizations began laying the foundation for vigorous local unions." Their leaders recognized that there was no point in avoiding the race issue; rather, through confronting it, by organizing African Americans, they could bring militant industrial unionism to the South, and with it a challenge to the white elites of sufficient dimension eventually to destroy them. They had most success in Alabama, where, by 1938, the United Mine Workers had signed up a hundred thousand southern members, mostly black. Food and tobacco unions had made some inroads in North Carolina, again amongst black workers. Important as these developments were, however, they were little more than pinpricks on the body of anti-labor sentiment in the South. In the years since 1914, challenges to the system had been easily repulsed. Black and white workers, kept apart by the caste system, were together only in the subordinate place they occupied in the socio-economic order.[10]

There were in the South individuals and groups not directly connected to the union movement, nor to millworker culture, who nevertheless were allies in labor's struggle for economic justice. Some, indeed, took the first slow steps towards advocating racial justice as well. In 1927 two young women, Louise McLaren and Lois McDonald, both with YWCA experience and a commitment to improving the lives of southern women caught up in the change from farm to factory, founded the Southern Summer School for Women Workers. As its historian, Mary Frederickson, has written, from 1927 to World War II the Southern Summer School provided young workers from textile, garment, and tobacco factories with the analytic tools for understanding the social context of their lives, the opportunity to develop solidarity with each other, and the confidence to participate fully in the emerging southern labor movement.[11]

Using graduates of the women's colleges of New England and the South, all with a commitment to bringing social and economic change to the region, as faculty, McDonald and McLaren aimed to give the young women who came each summer to Asheville, North Carolina, where the school was located, an understanding of the social and historical context of their own lives. Having achieved this awareness, they believed, their students could return to the mills and factories as active agents for change. Eventually the school worked closely with the CIO, providing training for local union activists. Though the school never attempted to enroll black students, faculty members were at pains always to stress the identical interests of black and white labor. Little known at the time, and almost forgotten now, the Southern Summer School was nevertheless one example of the radical impulse at work, aiming to reshape class and gender structures in the "solid South."

Another example was the Highlander Folk School. Highlander was the dream of Myles Horton, a young man from west Tennessee, who had studied in Denmark and became greatly influenced by the Scandinavian folk-school movement. He returned to the South in 1932, determined, in John Egerton's words, "to establish an institution of education and social activism for working-class adults in the mountains of Appalachia." He linked up with Don West, a Georgia farm boy with a theology degree and similarly radical educational notions, and they soon met Lilian Johnson, a wealthy Memphis woman who thought like them, and who agreed to lease them a property near Monteagle, Tennessee, which they could use as a school. Thus Highlander was born.[12]

West, the more radical of the two, soon departed, leaving Horton in sole control. He had hoped to use the school as a springboard to achieve racial change, but southern realities intervened. As in the summer school, Highlander's enrollees were white, and increasingly connected with the labor movement. Highlander's first years were economically precarious, but after the arrival of James Dombrowski, a Christian socialist with degrees from Emory University, Union Theological Seminary, and Columbia, and considerable managerial skills, it achieved a surprising degree of visibility in the South, especially among those determined to resist change. Though Horton soon had to abandon his hopes of challenging racial segregation, and Highlander's main concern became the improvement of the lot of white working people in the South, this was sufficient for it to become a prime focus for the opponents of southern progress. Moreover, Horton's tendency to forsake the classroom for periods of labor activism provided easy opportunities for attacking him. In 1932, for example, he joined the miners of Wilder, Tennessee, in their long strike against the Fentress Coal and Coke Company, and was arrested and jailed. His staff generally followed his activist example, resulting both in Highlander's visibility and in the vehemence of those who opposed its work.

As with the Southern Summer School, Highlander's fortunes became increasingly entwined with those of the CIO. It became affiliated with the new labor body in 1937 and committed itself completely to TWOC's drive to organize the textile industry. Most of its staff members and at least forty of its former students worked for the campaign. From then till after the war, Highlander was funded by the CIO and worked according to its direction. It became an important center for workers' education, and for the training of southern organizers. Like the Southern Summer School, Highlander hoped, through enabling workers to understand the context of their lives, to give them the means to change their lives. As Patricia Sullivan has pointed out, its "programs included workshops on labor history, union problems, labor legislation, public speaking, economics, and labor journalism" all designed to that end. By 1940, "Highlander alumni were among the leadership of national, regional, and local unions."[13]

Though the connection with the CIO gave Highlander a secure future, it also meant that the staff were unable to challenge racial segregation as directly as they had wished. Certainly they encouraged their students to confront their own prejudices in the interests of class and labor solidarity, and certainly they stressed the need to form biracial unions. But they were not able to integrate the campus until 1944—that would have been too much for the CIO's local leadership. They were only able to do so in 1944 at the expense of the former close relationship.

Highlander and the Southern Summer School were the two most important of the "alternative" schools aimed at bringing change to the South, but there were others. Commonwealth College, near Mena, Arkansas, was one such. Always known as a radical labor school, its head in the late 1930s was a fiery Presbyterian minister, the Reverend Claude Williams, who was almost certainly a secret member of the Communist Party. Its far left line became too much for the state authorities to stomach. They seized its property and closed it permanently in 1940. Ironically, as John Egerton has noted, one of its last enrolled students was Orval Faubus, later to gain notoriety as the governor who closed the schools of Little Rock in 1957 rather than let them be desegregated, and thus provoked a confrontation with federal power.[14]

The South's established universities and colleges were bastions of tradition and conservatism, the majority of the students being much more interested in sporting events and social activity than in political debate and social change. Nevertheless, there were a few who followed different drummers, who searched for means to cleanse the region of its racism and its rigid, class-based economic structure. At the University of Virginia, a young activist called Palmer Weber became "the primary catalyst of a small but vocal student movement that grew up around campus unrest during the early years of the depression."[15] In 1935 he even led a student delegation to the Virginia State House, in order to present a model bill calling, amongst more specific proposals, for an end to segregation in the South. The legislators were aghast, ordering the students from the chamber. This was the most dramatic action by a group of young dissenters who were always a tiny minority of their class but who were, nevertheless, quiet harbingers of changes to come.

The only southern university with claims to national status, and certainly the region's most liberal, was the University of North Carolina at Chapel Hill. Here, under the benign leadership of President Frank Graham, students and faculty were able to debate unpopular and unconventional ideas and positions and even engage in political action, with a freedom uncommon in the New South. The dramatist Paul Green, the publisher William T. Couch, even the sociologist Howard Odum encouraged students to challenge the certainties of their region—or most of them, for to debate segregation was still, in the main, off limits—and occasionally to take action against them. Green and Couch led a vigorous movement to secure justice for six textile workers jailed for conspiring to bomb the Holt Plaid Mill in Burlington during the

1934 textile strike, after a travesty of a trial. Although their activity was largely unsuccessful, it did lead to the formation of the Southern Committee for People's Rights, with the sociologist Olive Matthews Stone as its executive secretary. C. Vann Woodward, soon to become the South's most eminent historian, was a charter member. Again, though membership was small, the vision for the future was an enlarged one. At Vanderbilt University, too, the Reverend Alva Taylor, a passionate advocate of the social gospel, persuaded a handful of his students to share his social concerns, but in general southern colleges rarely challenged the status quo.

Student activism eventually led a few people, including Palmer Weber, to seek change through the Communist Party. Many more, however, sought it through the ceaseless advocacy of the Christian gospel's egalitarian message and attempted, in their own lives, to give it practical application. The group which best exemplified this perspective was the Fellowship of Southern Churchmen. Described by historian Robert F. Martin as "a loosely knit interdenominational and interracial association" of Christians who were "troubled by their region's mores" and "boldly sought to change them," the FSC existed from the mid-1930s to 1963. During that time this "little cadre of Christians" propounded "a radical critique of twentieth-century Southern civilization." It was primarily a discussion group, an agency through which Christians who felt deeply about the need for social and racial change in their region could maintain contact and develop a sense of community and common purpose, but its members, either individually or severally, at times engaged in direct action against the social structure long before it was politic, or remotely safe, to do so. Thus the FSC remained a bright beacon for the future.[16]

It was James Dombrowski, a young Christian socialist then working at Highlander, who took the initiative in forming the FSC. In May 1934, he invited like-minded "Liberals and progressive young ministers," to Monteagle, Tennessee, to hear the distinguished theologian Reinhold Niebuhr speak on "Religion and the Social Order." The response was reasonable; about eighty people attended, including a few blacks, and at the meeting's conclusion the group decided to form the Conference of Younger Churchmen of the South, primarily as a means of staying in touch. Among the group's leaders were Alva Taylor, Myles Horton, T. B. ("Scotty") Cowan, a flamboyant preacher and recent arrival from Scotland, and Howard Anderson ("Buck") Kester, the man who became the conference's first general secretary and gave it its initial purpose and direction.

Kester was one of the most remarkable figures in the history of southern radicalism. Born in Martinsville, Virginia, but raised in West Virginia, Kester seems to have been a rebel against the traditional views of his region and his family from an early age. After a period in YMCA work, he enrolled at the Vanderbilt University School of Religion, where he was profoundly influenced by Alva Taylor and Taylor's perspective on the social gospel. For the rest of his life this iconoclastic, passionate Christian socialist lived his version of Christian activism, constantly confronting the injustice and inequality of his region, brave, uncompromising, and totally committed. Best known for his role in the Southern Tenant Farmers Union, Kester worked with the embattled miners of Wilder, Tennessee, in 1932. In 1934 he went undercover for the National Association for the Advancement of Colored People (NAACP), investigating the brutal lynching of Claude Neal in Marianna, Florida, on its behalf, a risky assignment that almost cost him his life. In 1932 he had run for Congress on the Socialist Party ticket, and in 1934, when the Conference of Younger Churchmen was formed, he was working as field secretary of the Committee on Economic and Racial Justice, an organization headed by Niebuhr with the sole purpose of supporting Kester's work in the South. Once the CYC was formed (the name was changed to the FSC in 1936), the work of the two bodies merged.

FSC members, inspired by Kester, labored as individuals throughout the 1930s to change the South. Though they were bound together by a sense of common purpose and drew sustenance from this, their organization did not have even a rudimentary structural or administrative framework. In that sense, though it was a harbinger of the great postwar social revolution, the FSC bore little resemblance to the institutions that undergirded the later movement. Never a social action agency, it nevertheless provided a home for Christian men and women who wished, through the example of their lives, to cleanse the South of its interwoven class and racial biases.

Since the mid-1920s, other groups of white, mainly middle-class reformers had been working quietly in the South. They were often imbued with the ideals of the Progressive movement, and, without challenging the structures of segregation, they nevertheless aimed to ameliorate its worst excesses and injustices and to narrow the gulf between the races that it had created.

One such group was the Commission on Interracial Cooperation (CIC), formed in 1919 in reaction to the rebirth of the Ku Klux Klan and with the aim of uniting black and white leaders in the fight against racism. Under the leadership of a gentle Methodist pastor, Will Alexander, the CIC worked quietly throughout the 1920s, establishing hundreds of local groups throughout the South—black, white, and interracial—bringing together men and women who shared a concern at the increasing levels of racial violence in the region, especially the violence gratuitously meted out by white mobs to law-abiding black citizens. The CIC gathered information and disseminated countless news releases describing black achievements, as well as accounts of lynchings and Klan activism, to over a thousand newspapers and magazines.

Its ties to the intellectual community were important in bringing well-known college presidents like Wake Forest's William Louis Poteat and academic activists like Arthur Raper into the movement. Raper, a social scientist and another of the passionate liberals at the University of North Carolina, served as the CIC's research director. Indeed, the CIC commissioned the investigations that resulted in the publication in 1933 of his important book, *The Tragedy of Lynching*. Aware that the New Deal administration needed all the information it could get about the conditions of African Americans, the CIC also sponsored Raper's *Preface to Peasantry* (1936), and the 1939 study by Horace R. Cayton, an African American, and George Sinclair Mitchell, *Black Workers and the New Unions.*

The CIC recruited women to its ranks, those who had no wish to remain on the pedestal the South had erected in the name of honoring southern womanhood. Its women's director, the pugnacious Texan, Jessie Daniel Ames, founded and headed the influential Association of Southern Women for the Prevention of Lynching (ASWPL). When Alexander was called to Washington to head the Farm Security Administration—a New Deal agency that the CIC helped bring into action by its strong support in 1937 of the Bankhead-Jones Farm Tenancy Act—Ames in effect ran the CIC. Her enthusiasm breathed new life into many state and local interracial committees. By 1940, the ASWPL had signed up more than forty thousand southern women—mostly white—who had committed themselves to the ending of lynching, the worst of the South's race-based atrocities, and who deserve considerable credit for its steady decline during the 1930s. Scarcely a radical body, though many southern whites thought it so, and unwilling to challenge racial segregation even at its fringes, the CIC was nevertheless the only group working to moderate the destructive forces of racial violence during the height of the segregation era.

One agency that did begin to mount a challenge to segregation at this time was the NAACP. Though it was overwhelmingly northern-based in the interwar years, under the leadership of the energetic James Weldon Johnson some southern branches were established, the strongest being in Nashville and Atlanta. The agency's most important contribution at this time, however, was its role in training the young lawyers who would spearhead the first legal challenges to segregation's injustices. Of these, the first key figure was Charles H. Houston. Born in Washington in 1895, a member of the city's black middle class and the beneficiary of an excellent secondary education, Houston graduated from Harvard Law School in 1922 with a brilliant academic record and a determination to use his skills for the benefit of his race. After a brief apprenticeship in his father's Washington law firm, he joined the faculty of the Howard University Law School, becoming its vice-dean in 1929.

Houston transformed the law school "from a non accredited night school into a full-time, accredited program and created a laboratory for the development of civil rights law." The school became the training ground for a whole generation of young black lawyers, all committed to using the courts to secure racial justice and to the eventual ending of the southern caste system. Many of them came from the South, and together they would provide the NAACP's legal arm as it moved to challenge segregation in the courts. One of them, Thurgood Marshall, would eventually became the Supreme Court's first African American justice.[17]

In 1934 Houston left Howard to became the NAACP's full-time legal adviser. In this position his reputation grew steadily, especially after he had begun to argue cases in court himself. Indeed, he had appeared on the NAACP's behalf as early as 1932, defending George Crawford, an African American from Loudon County, Virginia, indicted for the murder of a wealthy white widow. In this case he challenged both the seating of the all-white jury, and the nature of the trial itself. He failed in both challenges, but his very appearance set a precedent. Moreover, Crawford was not, as was expected, sentenced to death but to life imprisonment. Jury members agreed that it was Houston's eloquent closing address that had swayed them.

Increasingly, however, Houston and his disciples argued cases that aimed at breaking down segregation, especially in public education. One of the first of these was *Gaines v. Canada*, which he argued himself. In 1935 the NAACP brought suit on behalf of Lloyd Gaines, who had been denied entry to the University of Missouri Law School because of his race. Instead he had been referred to the state-supported black college, Lincoln University, which had no law faculty; alternatively, he was told, he should go out of state. Houston argued that Missouri had a duty to provide

Gaines with a legal education equal to that of its white students, within the state's boundaries. The Missouri court ruled against him, but, two years later, by a six to two majority, the United States Supreme Court reversed the decision, accepting Houston's argument and directing the University of Missouri to admit Gaines. This was a path-breaking judgment, one on which precedents could be built in the long struggle to achieve legal sanction for an end to segregation. Thus the NAACP had joined the battle to change the South.

At the other end of the spectrum, so had the American Communist Party. The party had curtailed its southern activities after its disastrous failure in Gastonia in 1929, but in the maelstrom of the great depression the party leadership was directed to try again, this time working with the region's black dispossessed, conceding that the racism of the South's white textile workers was too formidable an obstacle to be overcome. In the 1930s the party made some inroads amongst Alabama's black steelworkers and miners, mainly in the Birmingham area. It was also active in Atlanta and Charlotte, working within the Workers Alliance, a union aiming to represent the unemployed. In the devastated southern countryside, the party was behind the Share Croppers' Union, a semi-underground, mainly black organization which eked out a half-life in Alabama during the 1930s, constantly threatened by the local law enforcement authorities. What distinguished the SCU was that its members were armed and, when attacked, shot back, most notably in Reeltown in Tallapoosa County, Alabama, as described by one of the survivors of the shoot-out, Nat Shaw (Ned Cobb). There, in December 1932, as SCU members grouped to prevent an eviction, they were involved in a firefight with the local sheriff and his deputies. When the shooting stopped, three were dead and several more wounded. Five SCU members, including Cobb, were subsequently jailed for their part in the affray, a boon to party propagandists, if not to the local farmers and farm workers. Nevertheless, the party, even in its failure, at least reached out to the black sharecroppers of rural Alabama and for a brief time inspired them to take action against those who oppressed them.

Communist lawyers provided noisy assistance to the defendants in a number of southern trials during the 1930s, most notably in the case of the nine young black men and boys accused of raping two white women in Scottsboro in 1931, a case that developed into the region's cause celebre during the years that followed. Communist lawyers also defended Angelo Herndon, another young African American, arrested at a rally in Atlanta and subsequently savagely sentenced for insurrection, and the white textile workers charged with the Burlington, North Carolina, bombing incident in 1934. They worked, too, within youth groups like the Southern Negro Youth Congress and the League of Young Southerners. Because of this work the party, despite its tiny membership, must be considered as one of the important groups challenging the southern political and social structure in the years before World War II.

The main activity of the American Socialist Party in the South during the 1930s was within the Southern Tenant Farmers Union. Organized by Howard Kester, H. L. Mitchell, the son of a sharecropper, and Clay East in 1934, with its strength mainly in Arkansas, the STFU, like the SCU, was an attempt through organization to confront the power structure of the Cotton Belt on behalf of the dispossessed tenant farmers and sharecroppers, though without the Alabama body's militance. By 1938 it had signed up more than thirty thousand members, black and white, many in integrated locals. Moreover, both black men and black and white women held local offices within the union. Though the white power structure, as always, proved too powerful, and the SFTU's successes were both limited and temporary, it, too, represented a challenge to the status quo, and, as such, another signpost to the future.

What of the nation's leaders? How far did the reforms of Franklin D. Roosevelt and the New Deal really impact on the South? In November 1934 the reporter Martha Gellhorn, then working for Harry Hopkins, head of the Federal Emergency Relief Agency (FERA), reported to her boss from Gastonia, North Carolina, in the wake of the unsuccessful textile strike, on the desperate situation of the region's unemployed. She described situations of real misery, but also spoke of the love the people had for the president, and of their reliance on him to lead them to a better future. In every home she visited, there was a picture of Roosevelt on the wall, usually clipped from a newspaper or magazine, but then lovingly framed. One woman in particular moved Gellhorn. This woman had been a mill worker but had not been taken back after the strike, and she was now trying to feed her family of five children on a weekly relief allowance of $3.40. "Her picture of the President was a small one," Gellhorn reported,

> and she told me her oldest daughter had been married some months before and had cried for the big colored picture as a wedding present. The children have no shoes and the woman is terrified of the coming cold as if it were a definite physical entity. There is practically no furniture left in the home, and you can imagine what and how they eat. But, she said, suddenly brightening, "I'd give my heart to see the President. I know he means to do everything he can for us; but they make it hard for him, they won't let him."[18]

Poor Southerners, white and black, were passionate supporters of the New Deal, despite the moderate nature of its reform program—there was no attempt to break down the southern caste system, for example, no challenge to segregation. Moreover, as we have seen, the provisions of the National Recovery Act brought little benefit to the textile workers who had placed so much faith in it. Nevertheless, for the region's dispossessed, the small farmers, the tenants and sharecroppers, and the unemployed of the cities and the mill villages, the New Deal relief schemes helped keep them alive. This was even true for black Southerners. As far as possible, most New Deal administrators did try to include African Americans within their programs; it was the first time the federal government had done so since Reconstruction.

Moreover, the New Deal enticed a host of Southerners to Washington, to work for the greatly expanded federal bureaucracy. Some, like the social worker Aubrey Williams, the lawyer Clark Foreman, and the CIC's Will Alexander, had long recognized the need for change in their native region, and hoped that the federal government might lead in the process. Others like the lawyer Clifford Durr found that the tragedy of depression and the new perspective provided by Washington work forced him to rethink his views on such fundamental issues as segregation. Outside government, Southerners like Lucy Randolph Mason of the National Consumers League, now working closely with federal agencies, also viewed the New Deal as the catalyst for regional change.

In 1938 a number of these young Southerners worked together to produce the Report on the Economic Conditions of the South, which Roosevelt used as his reason for declaring the South to be "the nation's number one economic problem," as he embarked on his largely unsuccessful attempt to influence the 1938 congressional elections in the region in favor of candidates who supported change.

The report was also the catalyst for the calling of a regional conference in November 1938, aimed at addressing a range of economic and social problems. The conference was the idea of Joseph Gelders, a leftist political activist from Alabama, and it was subsequently endorsed by a range of prominent and respectable individuals including Eleanor Roosevelt and eventually the president himself. It was held in Birmingham. More than twelve hundred delegates, 20 percent of whom were black, attended. They came from all walks of life, including businessmen, members of Congress, state legislators, federal officials, union leaders, lawyers, journalists, farmers, sharecroppers, professors, students, NAACP members, Democrats, socialists, even a few Communists. What they had in common was a recognition that the South's economic and social system was inefficient and unjust and had to be changed.

The formation of the Southern Conference for Human Welfare, as it came to be called, marked the first time these disparate elements for change had come together. For one of the delegates,

Virginia Durr, it was "a wonderful sort of love feast because it was the first time that all of these various elements from the South had gotten together. And we were not segregated."[19] For three days they discussed the South's myriad problems, using the report as their agenda. They had not meant to make segregation a particular issue, and it became so only after Birmingham's police chief, Eugene "Bull" Connor, forced it on them by requiring black and white delegates to sit apart. Mrs. Roosevelt, who was present, registered her disapproval by sitting in the aisle between the two sides. So emphatic was the mood of the conference that the delegates decided to form a permanent organization and to meet in general conference biennially. From then on, the SCHW was the agency through which most of the region's activists worked for reform. Perhaps never realizing the hopes of its inception, the SCHW's formation nevertheless represented a watershed in the South's journey towards racial and economic justice.

THE SOUTH AND THE ERA OF WAR

World War II brought unprecedented change to the South—as it did to the rest of the United States. John Egerton called it "a liberating war," and in terms of the enhanced opportunities it provided for the millions of people still ground down at its outset by the worst depression in modern times, he was clearly correct. First, the wartime economic boom not only ended the depression but also gave the South its first period of sustained and well-grounded economic growth since the Civil War. Tenant farmers and sharecroppers, men and women alike who had been tied to worn-out land, could now leave it, and they did so in the hundreds of thousands. Many left the region altogether for the factories, the shipyards, and the aircraft plants of the industrial heartland, for the Far West, for Detroit, for California, or for Seattle. Blacks in particular, as they had done during the earlier war, used the opportunity to get out from under segregation's oppressive weight.[20]

Most of those who left the farms, however, did not leave the South, but rather moved to the areas of opportunity within it, to the shipyards of Mobile, Alabama, and the other Gulf ports, to the textile mills, swamped with orders for uniforms, blankets, and other accoutrements of war, to the steel mills, the gas fields, and the coal mines, all crying out for labor, willing to pay wages the unions had fought fruitlessly for in peacetime and, gingerly, even willing to hire blacks, despite the white anger that usually ensued. Others serviced what became a crucial southern wartime industry—the military training camps. The region's space, its cheap labor supply, and its climate meant that by the end of the war more than 50 percent of the training camps were located there, providing another source of alternative employment for those who had left the land, as well as providing new and important markets for those remaining on it. Southern agriculture, too, participated in the wartime boom. Technical advances such as the mechanical cotton picker not only increased productivity but also contributed to the pool of available labor, as hand-picking became a thing of the past.

Southerners were on the move in another way, into the armed forces. More than two-thirds of America's black soldiers were from the South, as were one-third of the whites who served. Mixed with their patriotic motives for volunteering was the attraction of steady work and good pay, given their recent experience of unemployment and deprivation. Most of these men served abroad, and their perceptions were forever altered as a result. For black servicemen, the humiliation of serving in segregated units, the discrimination they encountered even as they fought to cleanse the world of racist regimes, and the stellar examples provided by those who beat the odds and proved themselves in battle combined to ensure there would be no willing return to the prewar caste system. A few of their white comrades, too, lost their racial prejudices in the crucible of conflict, returning home determined to change their region. World War II, then, changed the South's demography, altered its social and economic mold, and even affected its distinctive regional culture.

The change-making agencies that had struggled so hard in the depression South now had to adjust to the boom. The CIO, for example, and especially the TWUA found positive advantages in working with the National War Labor Board, the federal agency charged with regulating the wartime labor market, in compelling management to accept collective bargaining as the price of gaining lucrative government contracts. Wage rates in the mills doubled, as did the number of unionized plants. Textile workers lived better lives, an improvement gained, however, in unusual conditions, and more through government intervention than worker militancy, for most strikes were banned during the war years. Moreover, higher wages meant that for the first time southern millhands could join the consumer culture: they could own cars and could even begin buying a home. They had something to conserve, provided they kept working, and this could well pose problems for unions, who saw wage rates as only one aspect of the struggle for genuine industrial democracy.

The SCHW, which quickly developed strong links with the CIO, continued as the South's most activist biracial agency for change throughout the war. Before long, however, the spirit of unity which had characterized both the Birmingham meeting and its first year's existence was broken over the issue of Communist participation. Communists had been present at Birmingham; more importantly, a few had secured representation on SCHW subcommittees and used this to influence SCHW policy on a range of issues, especially America's attitude to the war in Europe, in which the Soviet Union was not yet involved. Though a resolution banning Communists from membership was watered down, the fight over ideological purity caused moderates and leftists alike to sever their connections with the conference.

Increasingly, the SCHW saw segregation as underpinning the myriad problems they had come together in 1938 to discuss. Its efforts throughout the war years, then, were directed towards ending segregation. In 1939 the SCHW began its campaign for the repeal of the poll tax, which had become, in Sullivan's words, "a potent symbol nationally of the undemocratic structure which supported the most powerful members of Congress." The poll tax discriminated against poor whites as well as blacks, but its prime purpose was to keep blacks from voting. It became, therefore, the focus for the SCHW's most effective campaign; and in the long run the philosophy that underpinned it, that political disfranchisement and segregation were both parts of the same whole, would be shown to be correct. Nevertheless the SCHW's direct focus on segregation alarmed some of its more moderate members, causing them to leave the agency.[21]

Some joined a gentler change-making body, one which grew out of the old CIC, and which argued that much could be accomplished without threatening segregation directly. This was the Southern Regional Council. The product of a series of segregated meetings "that aimed to broaden the dialogue among the CIC's constituency, the 'better class' of both races," and that explicitly excluded the participation of those deemed too closely tied to the New Deal, including Will Alexander himself, the participants represented a strain of southern liberalism that still accepted the caste system as a southern reality. As one of their number, the Atlanta journalist Ralph McGill, wrote in 1942, "Anyone with an ounce of common sense must see . . . that separation of the two races must be maintained in the South." Formally founded in Richmond in 1944, the SRC was soon to find out what SCHW's members already knew, that segregation lay at the root of all the South's tragedies. Nevertheless, its version of an interracial South was always less threatening than that of the SCHW.[22]

The federal government's regulatory agencies were also change-makers in the wartime South. The effect of the National War Labor Board has already been noted. Of equal significance was the Fair Employment Practices Commission (FEPC). Created by the president in 1941 in response to black pressure about discrimination in defense-related industries, the FEPC was always underfunded and lacked proper enforcement powers. Nevertheless, as the first federal agency since Reconstruction specifically devoted to racial issues, it was of vast symbolic importance. Moreover, in its investigatory capacity, the FEPC demonstrated such widespread patterns of discrimination in southern-based defense industries that some employers at least were shamed into modifying their work practices and using blacks in skilled positions, though the shortage of labor was always a more effective change-maker in this regard than the moral pressure of a federal agency. The vehemence with which defenders of white supremacy opposed the FEPC was, however, impressive testimony to its symbolic significance.

The NAACP grew in importance as an agency for change during the war years. The legal campaign waged by Houston and his disciples continued, but of equal significance was the rapid development of its regional and local base. This was largely due to the work of Ella Baker, southern field secretary at the time. A native of rural North Carolina, an organizer in Harlem during the depression, and a believer in grassroots collective action as a means of achieving change, Baker was instrumental in promoting branch activity. Traveling through the region, she took "the NAACP to churches, schools, barbershops and pool halls." She identified the needs of particular communities and built chapters round these. She made local people see that the NAACP could be an agency for change in their daily lives and could protect them from those who oppressed them. NAACP membership in the South in 1939 stood at 18,000. By 1945 it was 156,000. Ella Baker had much to do with this increase, and with the agency's local vitality and increasing militancy.[23]

For many southern liberals, the war's end promised a new beginning, a chance to cleanse the region of its unjust political and social systems. Aubrey Williams, who had returned home to Alabama, after the NYA, the agency he headed, had been terminated, to organize for the National Farmers Union, wrote of the "bottom-deep awakening" he sensed there; Lillian Smith found that her 1944 novel, *Strange Fruit*, about an interracial love affair, though banned in Boston, was being read enthusiastically by some of the residents of the small Georgia town where she had grown up. Franklin D. Roosevelt had been reelected in 1944 after a campaign in which he embraced an extension of the New Deal once peace was won. Moreover, he had spoken of a new world, one based on the four freedoms of the Atlantic Charter and moderated by a new supranational body, the United Nations. In such a new world, surely the "four freedoms" would also apply to the class inequalities and racial injustices remaining in the United States, or so Williams and his fellow progressives thought.[24]

First, there were encouraging signs that the South's monolithic political culture was cracking. In 1944 the former Rhodes scholar J. William Fulbright was elected senator from Arkansas, the most impressive of a group of younger politicians seeking and gaining power at federal and state levels. Others included Georgia's Governor Ellis Arnall, Senators Claude Pepper of Florida, Estes Kefauver and Albert Gore from Tennessee, and Senators Lister Hill and John Sparkman and Governor James Folsom of Alabama. These men had by no means abandoned the language of segregation, but they did mute its stridency and were much more inclined to talk of enlarging economic opportunities for all Southerners, white and black, than of a bright future for whites only. Moreover, they were often friendly to the CIO, welcoming its political support, again for some an indication that change through the political process was not impossible.

At the local level, too, there was also change, most notably an increase in black political participation. African Americans who had moved to the southern cities during the war to work in the shipyards and factories found it much easier to form associations and even to take part in local politics. By 1947 the percentage of eligible blacks registered to vote in the South, only 2 percent in 1940, had risen to 12 percent, and some local politicians, most notably William Hartsfield in Atlanta, recognizing the coming reality, began forming close alliances with the local black leadership. Again, liberals like Aubrey Williams viewed such gestures as pointing the way to a better future.

Moreover, some black servicemen, returning home after helping cleanse the world of Nazi racism, were in no mood to bend to segregation's injustices any longer. Some, like Aaron Henry and Medgar Evers in Mississippi, worked through the revitalized NAACP branches. Others simply attempted to exercise their rights individually, especially the right to vote, trying to win through the courts what the white power structure denied them. Their actions were brave, and some paid with their lives, but they persisted in the face of white hostility and judicial indifference. A few whites, however, supported them, students imbued with the ideals of the "four freedoms" and local groups of white veterans, their own mind-set altered by the war. In their actions, too, Williams saw glimpses of a better future.

The Fellowship of Southern Churchmen refocused both its activities and its membership at the end of the war. Moving its headquarters to the university town of Chapel Hill, North Carolina, it developed a solid organizational structure for the first time and began actively recruiting amongst the student body. Moreover, the FSC shifted its emphasis to programs involving local black communities; its work became explicitly interracial, confronting segregation directly. The SCHW, too, used the sense of possibility brought by peace to extend its activities. Specifically, it opened state branches throughout the South, hoping to establish firm links with other local agencies for change as well as to develop community programs of its own. It also emphasized its fund-raising activities, targeting in particular the "rich liberals" of New York—all positive signs for those hungry for social change.

Finally, the NAACP's lawyers continued to win courtroom battles, chipping away at the fabric of segregation. One of the most important occurred in 1944. Several years earlier the NAACP had broadened its sweep from education issues to include the franchise as well. Concentrating on the primary election, the only one that mattered in the one-party South, and one from which blacks had always been excluded, NAACP lawyers argued that to exclude blacks from this election was effectively to disfranchise one whole group of registered voters. On April 3, 1944, the Supreme Court agreed, striking down the white primary in *Smith v. Allwright*. The decision did not lead to a massive increase in black participation—there was still, after all, economic pressure and intimidation to deal with—but blacks now had the law on their side, and in time this would matter.

Of course, it would not be long before those who believed that the South was on the brink of change realized that they had greatly underestimated the strength of their opponents, and that the tide of history was not yet running their way. The first blow occurred even before V-E Day, when, on April 12, 1945, Franklin Roosevelt died suddenly. He had been their leader for so long, the towering lightning-rod and force for hope, that it had never occurred to southern progressives that he would not always be there to fulfill those functions and march with them towards a better future. Now he was gone, and in his place was someone they barely knew and instinctively distrusted, Harry S. Truman. He, after all, had replaced their hero, Henry Wallace, as vice president in 1945. They were wrong about Truman, who was to prove much more resolute in the cause of southern change than they had expected, and who in 1946 appointed the first ever Presidential Committee on Civil Rights, its brief to make recommendations aimed at securing racial justice for the South. Nevertheless, the transfer of presidential power was a bitter blow to those seeking southern change.

So, too, was the unfolding shape of the postwar world. Instead of an era of peace and global harmony, the world seemed to be sliding into a new and bitter type of war, as the wartime alliance between the United States and the Soviet Union unraveled and was replaced by an increasingly strident hostility, cloaked in the language of a struggle for world domination. It was rendered all the more terrifying by the prospect of nuclear struggle, as the devastation of a nuclear holocaust was now obvious to all after Hiroshima and Nagasaki. As attitudes hardened and peace gave way to the Cold War, the prospects for further social reform lessened. Moreover, those who opposed change, in the South and elsewhere, could always brand its advocates as Communists, adherents of an alien ideology. In such a climate of fear, the optimism of Aubrey Williams and his ilk was sadly misplaced.

The CIO soon found this out, as it prepared to move south with the aim of finally organizing the bulk of the South's industrial workers. Once more, the textile workers were the lynch pin.

"Operation Dixie" was what the CIO called its campaign, born out of the spirit of optimism at the war's end. Operation Dixie's organizers "targeted all major Southern industries in twelve different states," but the key industry was textiles. TWUA President Emil Rieve himself implanted the optimism of 1945. His union had enjoyed great success during the war, he claimed, and this would surely continue in peacetime. Southern workers would support the campaign, of that he was sure. There was "a spirit of victory" among them. Said CIO President Philip Murray, Operation Dixie would serve as a "beacon light to all unorganized workers."[25]

Such boundless optimism was soon shown to be unjustified. TWUA organizers, the bulk of Operation Dixie's strike force, were as ill-prepared as prewar organizers had been for the intransigence of southern management, its determination to resist all attempts to reduce its authority, even if it meant breaking the law. Most accounts of the organizing drive's failure list this as the main cause. Barbara Griffith, for example, claims the drive failed because "workers in company-owned mill villages in the American South lived under the most debasing kind of police tyranny." Manufacturers constantly raised the twin specters of Communism and race-mixing against the organizers, despite the fact that the TWUA was one of the most fiercely anti-Communist of all CIO unions. Manufacturers wrote to workers emphasizing the immigrant origins of the union's leadership, used overtly anti-Semitic language, and constantly stressed that the CIO's cautious stand on racial equality masked a determination to drag blacks into the mills at the expense of white workers. To a workforce that often saw no dichotomy between Klan and union membership, this was always a potent argument. The continued power of the South's ruling power structure, together with its ability to appeal to regional prejudices, was a potent reason for Operation Dixie's failure.[26]

To this must be added the views of the mill workers themselves. For many, the memory of 1934 was still powerful. The failure of the strike then, the inability of the union to assist the workers in any material way, and the ferocity of the owners' revenge all made them wary of going down that path again. Moreover, mill workers had made great gains economically during the war and were continuing to make them. They had a little money for the first time in their lives and could look beyond life's barest necessities to the purchase of a car, a refrigerator or record player, even a home—all on the installment plan, of course. To get mixed up in a union again, and certainly to be involved in strike action, would jeopardize all this. Finally, it could be argued that by concentrating on textiles and white workers the CIO missed its opportunity in the South, for it was in industries such as lumber, pulp and paper, and tobacco and food processing—industries where large numbers of blacks worked—that union enthusiasm was at its greatest. Whatever the reason, Operation Dixie did not transform the South in the immediate postwar years, and the South has been hostile territory for organized labor ever since.

Those brave black men and women who sought to bring change through demanding their individual rights found that doing so was to invite intimidation, violence, and sometimes death. Most blacks knew of the fate of Isaac Woodard who in February 1946, still in his Army uniform, was dragged from a bus in Batesburg, South Carolina, after an altercation with the driver, and blinded by police billy clubs. Later that month, in Columbia, Tennessee, a full-scale race riot broke out after a dispute between a department store clerk and a black navy veteran and his mother. In July and August that year, at least a dozen African Americans were lynched in the Deep South, the majority of them veterans, including Maceo Snipes, who was killed in Butler, Georgia, after registering to vote, the first black in the county to do so. Whites, concerned that black veterans in particular were stepping "out of their place," and thus providing examples that could not be permitted to continue, turned, as they had always done, to violence as their means of preventing change. They were secure in the knowledge that they were safe from the scrutiny of local law enforcement authorities. Indeed, in one of the most brutal of these racial murders, the shooting of two young couples—one of the men a veteran—in Walton County, Georgia, by a mob of two dozen whites, a state trooper was at the scene. In the face of such violence, men like Medgar Evers and George Elmore worked quietly within the local ranks of the NAACP, preparing the groundwork for an assault on the system when the climate was more propitious. Aubrey Williams's belief that they would form an irresistible shock-wave for change was, again, incorrect.

Then, too, most of the liberal politicians had a short shelf life. Governors like Ellis Arnall of Georgia, James Folsom in Alabama, and Earl Long in Louisiana were either defeated at the polls by resurgent opponents or found their efforts nullified by statehouse opposition. Neither Folsom, first elected governor of Alabama in 1946, nor Long, first elected in 1948, were integrationists, but as Numan Bartley has pointed out, both "rejected much of the mythology and practice of white supremacy." In a sense, both were in the populist tradition, claiming to govern in the name of "the people," which included blacks as well as whites, and which emphasized class-based issues. Both, as Bartley notes, "seemed perplexed by the depth of hostility white supremacists displayed towards black people" in the postwar South, and both saw moral as well as political reasons for treating blacks decently. "If these colored people helped build this country," Long once mused, "if they could fight in its army, then I'm for giving them the vote." Both were out of touch with the South's hardening racial climate, and both were eventually consigned to electoral oblivion, defeated by reality like other optimists.[27]

In Washington, men like William Fulbright, Lister Hill, and John Sparkman read the message more expertly. Once considered the hope of their region's liberal wing, they all moved steadily to the right and, in particular, became outspoken defenders of "the Southern way of life." Though some of them became experts in other areas—Fulbright in foreign policy, Hill in health—they steadfastly defended segregation alongside overt racists like Mississippi's Theodore Bilbo and James Eastland and in other ways retreated from their liberal roots. Only Lyndon Johnson managed to keep at least a toe in the liberal camp on the race issue while rapidly ascending the ladder of power.

Those social action groups outside mainstream politics that had greeted the peace with such optimism in 1945 also found their reach sadly shortened. The FSC's program of community activism, in partnership with local blacks, was usually thwarted by white community resistance. An FSC project in Tyrell County, North Carolina, in 1947 to build a community store was violently broken up by local whites because the FSC group included a black student. In Atlanta, an interracial work project suffered a similar fate. By 1949 the FSC had decided to abandon all interracial work, and, indeed, to relocate from Chapel Hill to Buckeye Cove in the North Carolina mountains. There it struggled on for the rest of the 1950s, mainly as a summer retreat, before winding up its affairs, a lonely organization that had helped create a climate for change, but was now bypassed by time.

The SCHW, similarly, lost focus and support in the changing South. The Communist issue returned to haunt it in the hardening Cold War climate. In 1947 the House Un-American Activities Committee labeled it "perhaps the most deviously camouflaged Communist-front organization" in the nation, the CIO withdrew all financial support from it, and several long-term members like Lucy Randolph Mason quit the agency. In response, SCHW President Clark Foreman moved it even further to the left. He decided that the conference should back Henry Wallace and his Progressive Party in his bid from the left to unseat Truman in 1948. Indeed, SCHW members helped organize Wallace's southern tour in the fall, when he bravely advocated desegregation before jeering multitudes, especially in North Carolina. Nevertheless, the decision to support him ruined the SCHW. As remaining New Deal liberals like Williams and Clifford Durr withdrew their support, unwilling to reject the party of FDR, the charges of the Red-baiters looked less ridiculous, while Wallace ran even more poorly in the South than elsewhere. Shortly after the election the SCHW announced that the conference was suspending operations, with the high hopes of 1938 largely unfulfilled.[28]

Truman and the Democrats were challenged by another political group in 1948, the States' Rights Democrats—or Dixiecrats as they quickly became known. The Dixiecrats were Southern Democrats who broke with the president and the national party over the issue of a civil rights plank in the national party platform. Truman's Committee on Civil Rights had reported in 1947, recommending "the elimination of segregation based on race, color, creed or national origin," from American life, and when the president endorsed its specific proposals in a message to Congress, anguished southern conservatives prepared to leave the party. When the Democratic National Convention refused to adopt a states' rights plank in its platform and Truman received the nomination, States' Rights Democrats resolved to hold their own convention. Meeting in Birmingham, they nominated South Carolina's governor, J. Strom Thurmond, as their presidential hope and Mississippi's Governor Fielding Wright as his deputy. In so doing, they hoped to deny the South to Truman, thus ensuring his defeat and teaching the national party that southern beliefs and practices were not to be tampered with. Profoundly conservative in philosophy, the Dixiecrats were a testament to the continuing strength of the traditional leadership.

The Dixiecrats, however, failed in their aim. Though Thurmond carried four states, Alabama, Mississippi, South Carolina, and Louisiana, it was not enough to influence the result. Truman was elected, carrying the rest of the South. Nevertheless, the movement had had some effect. Most of the regular Democrats returned to Congress from the South were vehemently opposed to their party's civil rights platform, and Truman himself showed little interest in translating intent into legislation. The civil rights platform remained a harbinger of the future, rather than something to be translated into legislation as a matter of urgency. Again, this signified an end to the optimism of 1945.

Still, there was always the court system, and here the NAACP continued to make steady progress, challenging segregation in the courts, still mainly in the area of equal access to public education but also in other areas where the opportunity arose. Of the team Houston had trained, it was now Thurgood Marshall who had become the acknowledged leader. In 1940 he had argued an important case before the United States Court of Appeals challenging salary differentials between black and white teachers in the Norfolk, Virginia, school system. Over the next decade he argued many other cases, adding to his reputation as the NAACP's top civil rights lawyer, but, more importantly, also adding to the legal "chain of precedent" on which future victories would be built.

One of the most important cases was *McLaurin v. Oklahoma State Regents for Higher Education*, in 1948. George McLaurin, an elderly black teacher, having been granted entry, through court action, to the University of Oklahoma's Graduate School of Education, was then kept separate from the other students, even being forced to confine himself to a roped-off area in the library. Marshall, therefore, went back to court, arguing that to treat McLaurin in this way was to confer on him a "badge of inferiority which affected his relationship, both to his fellow students and his professors." In 1950 the Supreme Court agreed with him, asserting that equality of treatment had to be real, that mere entry into a previously whites-only facility was not enough. Carefully considering the language of this and two analogous judgments, and noting that in all of them the Court had been unanimous, Marshall and his team decided it was time to stop challenging individual cases of unequal facilities but instead to force the Court to confront the legality of segregation itself—not just the deficiencies of its implementation.

The NAACP had the legal tools at hand. In Clarendon County, South Carolina, the local NAACP leader, Reverend J. A. De Laine, had mounted a challenge to the county's segregated school system, and Marshall decided to use this to shift the educational battleground from graduate and professional education to the ordinary schools of the South and to broaden the target so much that it became segregation itself. The case, *Briggs v. Elliot*, was first heard in 1951. From the start, NAACP lawyers attacked segregation, arguing that the damage inherent in forced racial separation could never be ameliorated by the provision of equal facilities. As expected, Marshall lost in the district court, but everyone knew that it was the Supreme Court that would decide the issue.

On its way there, a number of other cases, all challenging segregation in public schools, were joined with it. One such had begun after Oliver Brown, a welder and minister from Topeka, Kansas, had been refused permission to enroll his daughter in one of the city's whites-only schools. He therefore brought suit, assisted by the NAACP, and when the Supreme Court decided to hear all similar cases under the one label, it was Brown's case that was chosen, in *Brown v. the Board of Education of Topeka, Kansas.*

The Supreme Court began its deliberations in December 1952. Argument and deliberations continued in the first months of 1953, until the sudden death of the chief justice, Fred M. Vinson. When the court reconvened in the fall of 1953, it was under the leadership of California's former governor, Earl Warren. The NAACP, by this time, had added two well-known historians to its team, one white, one black, and both Southerners—John Hope Franklin and C. Vann Woodward. Their job was to instruct the justices on the context of segregation and in particular to convince them that this was no age-old folkway, but rather a practice arising from the unsettled situation of the post–Civil War South. The judges also heard from sociologists and psychologists, who emphasized the inherently destructive effect of segregation on the attitudes of young children. Nevertheless, its legal defenders had powerful arguments based on precedent on their side, and when the session closed in December 1953, both sides hoped for victory.

It was not until May 17, 1954, that Warren announced the Court's unanimous decision, perhaps its most important single judgment in the twentieth century. In it, the Supreme Court declared its belief that in the field of public education, the doctrine of "separate but equal had no place. Separate educational facilities are inherently unequal." Nothing would be the same after *Brown.* The struggle for southern change would intensify in the years ahead and would increasingly focus on the life and work of its greatest leader, Martin Luther King. Under King, ideas and action would come together and would change both the region and the nation.

THE CIVIL RIGHTS REVOLUTION

Mrs. Rosa Parks could have had no idea, as she waited for her regular bus on December 1, 1955, that she was about to be responsible for the "precipitating moment" in America's most far-reaching social movement, the southern civil rights revolution, nor that her actions would soon thrust a young Baptist preacher, the Reverend Martin Luther King, into the spotlight of national leadership. A seamstress in Montgomery, Alabama, and well respected in that city's African American community, Mrs. Parks was also secretary of the local NAACP chapter, a friend of the town's leading black activist and NAACP president, E. D. Nixon, and, as such, an individual committed to changing the South's social system. She was about to play a crucial role in the growing drive to do so.

As the bus filled up, those seats reserved for whites at the front were soon taken. With four white passengers standing, the driver instructed the four black riders seated immediately behind the white section, one of whom was Mrs. Parks, to vacate their seats. She alone refused to do so. After repeated warnings, she was arrested, charged with violation of the city's segregation ordinances, and taken to jail, where E. D. Nixon quickly posted her bond. The local NAACP had been looking for such an incident for some time, aiming to use it to test segregation on the city's bus lines. Mrs. Parks agreed to go along with this aim and with that left her mark on the story of southern change.

As word of her arrest spread throughout Montgomery's black community, Nixon and his advisers decided to channel the spirit of anger thus aroused into a specific protest against segregation on Montgomery's buses. Deciding on a one-day boycott the following Monday, they spread the word mainly through the pulpit at Sunday services. The next day the buses ran empty as thousands of blacks walked or hitched rides to workplaces and schools, in dramatic protest against the indignities of their everyday lives.

The success of the boycott astounded its organizers, so much so that they decided to continue it indefinitely. This would necessitate a regular organization, however, and more importantly a designated leader, someone to coordinate the boycott, to act as spokesperson and negotiator, and to rally flagging spirits in the difficult months ahead. After some discussion, local leaders turned to a young Baptist preacher, recently arrived in town to take over the Dexter Avenue Church, for the job. As he had no roots in Montgomery, they reasoned, and belonged to no group or faction, he would have less trouble than others in holding the community together; moreover, this would make it easier for him to leave if everything turned sour. Thus Martin Luther King, perhaps the greatest of all southern activists, took his place in American history. In a speech at the boycott's inaugural night, his first as leader of the Montgomery Improvement Association, he set the tone for the next decade. He spoke of the coming of a time "when people get tired of being trampled over by the iron feet of oppression," when they raise up the "weapon of protest." Protest, however, must be without violence, it must accord with the spirit of the Gospels and "the name of Christian love," and its end must be justice for all, till it "runs down like water, and righteousness like a mighty stream." Thus Martin Luther King defined the cadences of, and the philosophy behind, his branch of civil rights activism. These were both biblical, and in that sense the Civil Rights Movement was the last great Christian revolutionary movement. Leaders and followers alike battled the evil of segregation with the social justice notions of the Christian Gospels uppermost in their minds.

King was no scion of poverty; he came from as privileged a position as was possible for a southern black man. Born in Atlanta, the son and grandson of clergymen on both sides of his family, respected members of the city's upper middle class, he was reasonably well protected from segregation's worst excesses. He had moved North for his theological training and at the time of the boycott was completing his doctorate at Boston University. His theological training had left him deeply imbued with the ideals of the social gospel and the possibilities of creating the kingdom of God on earth, as well as introducing him to the ideas of Mohandas Gandhi, the great Indian exemplar of nonviolent resistance to injustice. Moreover Reinhold Niebuhr had taught him about the powerful presence of evil in the world. As he embarked on his career as activist, therefore, with a lofty ideal before him, King had no illusions about the difficulty of achieving it.

For over a year, Montgomery's African American citizens stayed off the city's buses, and more than anything else it was King's leadership that gave them the strength to sustain the effort. Throughout the bus boycott, the symbolic beginning of the Civil Rights Movement, he was the inspiration. His Christian rhetoric and his courage symbolized both the spirit and the determination of people's resistance. If, finally, it was the Supreme Court that brought the boycott to its end by finding segregation on buses unconstitutional, it was Martin Luther King who had first shown southern blacks that through collective action they could confront the white power structure and win. Moreover, he had given them an ideology, active nonviolence in a spirit of Christian love, through which to wage the war.

And it would be a long struggle. Though a few southern whites, often liberal survivors of the SCHW like Aubrey Williams and Clifford and Virginia Durr, lent King quiet but valuable support, the city's white community resisted even the most moderate of proposals for change with a ferocity that initially surprised even King, and that indicated just how intransigent the white South was and with what vehemence it would defend its "way of life." Nevertheless, when on December 21, 1956, Martin Luther King boarded a local bus and sat in the front seat, it was a profound moment in the history of southern activism.

By this time, King had achieved national recognition as the most important new figure in black America. He would never again belong only to Montgomery and indeed left the city in 1959 for Atlanta to superintend more closely the affairs of the Southern

Christian Leadership Conference (SCLC), the civil rights agency he had founded in the wake of the boycott's success and through which he would work thereafter. Moreover in those years he thought deeply about the efficacy of nonviolence, eventually combining his Christian principles, his knowledge of Gandhi's teaching, and his understanding of the power of militant mass protest into the ideology of nonviolent direct action which would so dominate his wing of the southern Civil Rights Movement. His message was one of no compromise with the evil of white supremacy while at the same time eschewing all hatred for those who practiced it. Evil, violent evil, had to be confronted, but only through nonviolent means; to do or think otherwise was merely to emulate the evildoers. Not everyone agreed with King philosophically, and many more people could not contain themselves in practice, but the fact remains that he provided, in nonviolent direct action, the spiritual and ideological means for southern blacks to fight for their freedom while at the same time exciting the imagination, and in time the commitment, of thousands of white supporters. His was a magnificent achievement.[29]

Among the tens of thousands King touched was a group of freshmen attending North Carolina's all-black Agricultural and Technical College in Greensboro. Often from the best black high school in the city, imbued with a pride in their race and the great ideals of liberal democracy, they were also reminded daily of the injustices and indignities of segregation. Moreover, they had eagerly debated the ideas of Martin Luther King and rejoiced in the example of Montgomery. When one of them, Joseph McNeil, was refused service at a Greensboro hamburger stand, they decided to take some direct action of their own and in so doing moved the Civil Rights Movement into a new phase. The next day, McNeil and three other freshmen went to the local Woolworth's store, made a few purchases, and then sat at the lunch counter. Denied service, they refused to leave, as a hostile crowd gathered. They remained until the store closed, vowing to return the next day, which they did, along with twenty-three others, young men and women from local black colleges. By the end of the week some white students had joined, and the "sit-in" movement had begun. Like the Montgomery bus boycotters, these young people were deeply imbued with the spirit of nonviolent direct action—in that sense they were King's disciples. Yet the movement was a spontaneous one, King himself had neither sparked it off, nor did he control it as it spread. It was a classic example of the translation of ideas into social action.

Had the members of Greensboro's local power structure negotiated promptly with the young demonstrators, perhaps the sit-in movement might have ended there. But they did not, and as a consequence thousands of young Southerners, men and women, white and black, sat in at lunch counters and store restaurants throughout the region in the summer of 1960. The Greensboro demonstrations remained relatively violence-free, but this was not so in other communities. In Nashville, for example, police allowed white hecklers the latitude to beat and kick students from Fisk and Vanderbilt Universities as they crowded downtown lunch counters. In most cases, however, violence was counterproductive, simply galvanizing the local black community into supporting the young activists. This is what happened in Greensboro after authorities had forty-five demonstrators arrested. Local black leaders organized a boycott of city stores to such good effect that six months after McNeil and his friends first made their statement, all downtown lunch counters had been desegregated. In Nashville, and in many other cities, blacks eventually won the right to eat in the stores they shopped in. Young black people had taken the lead. Radicalized by the ideas of Martin Luther King, impatient with the slow process of legal redress, they had confronted white supremacy directly and had won a victory that symbolized much more than the right to eat a store hamburger or hot dog if they chose to. Moreover, the sit-in movement sparked the creation of the Student Non-Violent Co-ordinating Committee (SNCC), a permanent organization of young activists working for change at the local level and a key player in the struggles ahead. Initially the product of Martin King's ideas, SNCC members eventually became disillusioned with nonviolence and Christian love and with King's leadership itself.

The next phase of the civil rights struggle also involved young people and, like the sit-ins, owed much to King's ideas but little to his direct involvement. The Congress of Racial Equality (CORE) had been created in 1942 with a commitment to nonviolent direct action that obviously predated King's. As early as 1947 CORE attempted to test the Supreme Court's recent ban on segregation on interstate public transport in the South by sending interracial teams of riders into the region, but the effort was thwarted by local police. In 1961 CORE decided to try again, since the Supreme Court had extended its ban to include terminal facilities as well. Under the direction of James Farmer, from May 1961 teams of riders were sent southwards to ride the Trailways and Greyhound buses of the region.

The riders met little resistance in the upper South, but it was a different tale in Alabama. On May 14 those on the Greyhound bus were attacked near Anniston by a mob that set the bus alight, and the riders were lucky to escape with their lives. The Trailways riders made it to Birmingham, where they were attacked by an angry crowd waiting at the terminal, while the local police were strangely absent. Despite the violence, those riders still physically able to do so planned to continue to Montgomery, but neither of the bus lines would carry them. Instead, the Justice Department flew them to New Orleans; the CORE-sponsored "Freedom Ride" was over.

Yet the journeying continued, as members of the newly formed SNCC stepped into the breach. Twenty-one young veterans of the "sit-in" movement, mainly from Nashville, traveled to Birmingham, determined to complete the ride to Montgomery. After some delay, they set out on May 20, accompanied by an array of police cars and helicopters. The two-hour journey passed without incident, and all was quiet at the bus terminal—threateningly so. The riders carefully alighted, but as they did so people poured out of the surrounding buildings in an obviously carefully orchestrated move, as Justice Department observers watched, powerless and bewildered. There were, however, no police to check the mob as its members brutally attacked the activists. When it was over, every single rider needed hospital treatment and the incident had made national news.

Only then did Martin Luther King arrive in Montgomery, there to give aid and comfort to the injured. The government, too, decided it could no longer tolerate defiance of federal law, sending four hundred marshals to Montgomery to encourage the city's future compliance. The riders, their numbers augmented by fresh SNCC volunteers, continued to Jackson, Mississippi, where there was no mob awaiting them. Instead, they were promptly arrested and sent to jail, the result of a deal between the attorney general, Robert F. Kennedy, and Mississippi's powerful Senator James O. Eastland. All that summer, however, the riders came, until, again, the government was forced to act. On September 22 the Interstate Commerce Commission issued a new set of rules covering interstate transport, including compliance provisions that made continued defiance impossible. The "Freedom Riders" had won their battle.

In winning this campaign, CORE and SNCC had established themselves as frontline civil rights agencies, challenging King's SCLC for control of the movement. Moreover both the "sit-ins" and the "Freedom Rides" had shown that segregation could be successfully opposed, even in the Deep South, provided that confrontation could be provoked of such a dimension that the federal authorities had no choice but to intervene. Increasingly, this became the tactical underpinning for future action— seek out the most racist of the white power structures, provoke them into violence, and hope that the consequent national outcry would ensure swift government action.

If new agencies for change, like CORE and SNCC, increased in strength as the social revolution quickened its pace, the older white-led liberal groups like the FSC and the SCHW's successor, the Southern Conference Educational Fund, withered away, their job done, their funding sources dry. Old-style liberals like Aubrey Williams, and even Lillian Smith, while entirely sympathetic to the new activism, struggled to find places within the new agencies it had generated and generally ended up, already half-forgotten, cheering from the sidelines.

Of course, the importance of the NAACP's legal work remained undiminished, even as direct challenges to segregation increased. The white South did not accept the *Brown* decision; instead they perfected plans for its evasion, as the initial euphoria of the South's blacks evaporated before the grim realization that the battle was just beginning. Those disposed to resist change were given encouragement, too, by President Eisenhower's pointed refusal to endorse the Court's decision and insist on its compliance. Had he thrown the full moral authority of the presidency behind the Court, most observers believed that moderate Southerners might well have prevailed, and desegregation would have occurred, albeit reluctantly. But he did not, and into the leadership vacuum thus created came the racists of the white South, determined on "no surrender." By 1956, membership of the White Citizens Council was on the rise; in the years ahead the WCC would effectively control local government in the rural South, violently resisting any desegregation proposals, no matter how mild, and intimidating those blacks bold enough to support them. It was as if nothing had changed, as once again the NAACP took to the courts.[30]

It was a hard battle. In 1956 NAACP lawyers failed in their attempt to have Autherine Lucy enrolled as the University of Alabama's first black student, despite court decisions in their favor. University authorities expelled her nonetheless, following widespread mob disorder. The following year, however, when a mob in Little Rock, Arkansas, successfully prevented the court-ordered integration of Central High School, the NAACP eventually won the battle. Arkansas Governor Orval Faubus chose to defy the court for political reasons, in what was to become the most important challenge to *Brown v. the Board of Education*.

After increasing violence, during which howling mobs of whites threatened the lives of the nine black students chosen to integrate the school, and one, Elizabeth Eckford, came very close to being lynched, President Eisenhower sent federal troops to enforce compliance. Soldiers guarded the students throughout the school year and did what they could to prevent at least some of the acts of personal harassment that became part of the students' daily lives. Eight of the nine students stuck it out. Faubus closed all of Little Rock's schools the next year, in a further act of defiance, though local pressure soon forced him to quietly reopen them. By sending in the troops, however, Eisenhower had provided a model for federal action that his successor, John F. Kennedy, would reluctantly follow.

In 1962, James H. Meredith, a black air force veteran, won the right to enter the University of Mississippi, again through the work of the NAACP's legal team. As in the Little Rock crisis, state authorities, led by Governor Ross Barnett, refused to comply. Extensive negotiations between the president and Barnett were fruitless, and after a night of violence that left two dead and 160 federal marshals injured, Kennedy, like Eisenhower, sent in the troops, who ensured Meredith's entry and protected him throughout his stay at "Ole Miss." Troops were also needed to ensure the integration of the University of Alabama the following year, though this time violence was averted due to Governor George Wallace's surly recognition of the inevitable. These three confrontations, however, each illustrated the intransigence of the white South. Enforcement of the *Brown* decision had to be fought for every inch of the way, whether against outright defiance or against legal subterfuge. Moreover, ten years after its promulgation, just over 1 percent of black schoolchildren in the old Confederacy attended school with whites—far from the "all deliberate speed" the Supreme Court had mandated in 1955. Where there had been progress, it had overwhelmingly been in the border states, in cities like Topeka that were hardly southern, or in parochial school systems. The Deep South remained defiant. It was the very slowness of court procedures, the lack of certainty that favorable decisions would be enforced, and the seeming reluctance of the federal government to act decisively until severely pushed that prompted an increasing reliance on direct action, as African American Southerners found their patience running out.

Martin Luther King doubtless felt this way as he traveled to Albany, in southwest Georgia, in December 1961, there to assist

SNCC activists in an all-out campaign against segregation, which after a year seemed to be going nowhere in the town. Thousands of blacks had marched, had "sat-in," had attempted to register to vote, and had filled the area's jails. Yet nothing had changed. Why?

One reason was that the town's chief of police, Laurie Pritchett, was a highly intelligent man who had read King's work and knew how important gaining national attention was to the success of a direct-action campaign. Without it, there was no pressure for government action or even local negotiation. The key to such publicity was the provocation of violence—the sight of brutal police and violent whites attacking peaceful demonstrators always excited the media. Pritchett decided, therefore, that while there would be plenty of arrests in Albany, there would be no police brutality. For nearly a year his policy worked, hence the call for Dr. King and the national attention his presence in the town was bound to provide.

Certainly, King's presence in Albany made the network news, for he and his deputy Ralph Abernethy had been there only a day or so before they were sent to jail—for marching without a permit. Yet even this symbolic act failed in its purpose, partly because they did not stay in jail for long, quickly accepting bail, but also because King's very presence in Albany brought to a head simmering tensions in the town between those who had favored outside support and those who continued to emphasize the Albany movement's local nature. Nevertheless, though he quickly left the town, King would remain connected to it. He and Abernethy faced trial in February 1962 on charges arising from their December arrests. They were both found guilty, fined $178, and sentenced to forty-five days in jail in default of payment. They planned to serve their sentence in full, hoping that finally the Albany movement would receive sustained national attention as a result. But again they were thwarted. Quietly Chief Pritchett arranged for the payment of their fines; bewildered, the two men left the town, the local movement soon petered out, and King and the SCLC lost prestige as a result. Mass action in Albany had failed.

Nevertheless, the lessons learned in Albany would be put to good use a year later in Birmingham, Alabama, a city where recent acts of racial violence had earned it the sobriquet of "Bombingham." First, there was no point in challenging a moderate police chief like Pritchett, who was determined to avoid confrontation, rather than someone who actively sought it, as Birmingham's "Bull" Connor habitually did. Second, Albany had no moderate business community, willing to negotiate with demonstrators as the price for social peace. Birmingham possessed one, led by lawyer David Vann. Birmingham also had a dedicated local civil rights group, of which the Reverend Fred Shuttlesworth was the acknowledged head. Most importantly, King now understood that the South would not change without federal action. This must be the purpose of all future mass demonstrations, to create a national consensus for change that the government could not resist. The federal government, in other words, must itself become an active agent for change, if the South was to be transformed. Birmingham accordingly was selected as the site for the first such confrontation.

King and his team arrived there in early April 1963, and a well-planned program of economic boycotts, mass meetings, and peaceful demonstrations began. Initially Connor kept calm, to the extent that the SCLC leadership worried that it might be Albany all over again. There was a change, though, on April 12, when King himself was arrested, Connor's control having finally snapped. He turned the city's police dogs on marchers, giving the nation's media the first of many pictures of official violence in the city. Meanwhile, in jail, and in response to a reproving letter from eight local clergymen, King wrote his most famous tract. His moving "Letter from Birmingham Jail" was published throughout the land, legitimizing the Birmingham campaign as no single piece of writing had done before. The "Letter" remains one of the classic statements of higher purpose in the sweep of American history.

The "Letter from Birmingham Jail" had no effect on "Bull" Connor, even as it focused national attention on his city, and support for the marchers grew throughout the nation. In a move that shocked even some of his supporters, King decided to turn Birmingham's school children into frontline demonstrators. The nation watched aghast as Connor, now out of control, turned the city's dogs and high-pressure fire hoses on wave upon wave of young marchers. The city's moderate business leaders, as their carefully fashioned progressive veneer collapsed about them, started to negotiate seriously. On May 10 an accord was announced that began the process of desegregation in this, the most racially divided of southern cities. It was, said Dr. King, "the most magnificent victory for justice we've ever seen in the Deep South."

It was also an example for blacks across the region to follow. There were "little Birminghams" throughout the South in the summer of 1963, as blacks demonstrated a new pride and assertiveness, a determination not to be fobbed off with tokenism ever again. Martin Luther King had become the unchallenged leader of the Civil Rights Movement, and nonviolent direct action had become its ideology. The failure in Albany was now far behind him.

King later wrote that the sound of the explosion in Birmingham reached all the way to Washington, and certainly the most important consequence of the summer of 1963 was that President Kennedy finally realized that the federal government must join the movement, that it, too, had a role to play in the drive for social change. Accordingly, on June 11, 1963, he announced on national television his plan to send to Congress the most comprehensive civil rights bill in American history, one that would cleanse the South of many vestiges of segregation, especially those that had been the targets of recent direct action—public accommodations, the schools, and economic discrimination. The language of the speech signaled his commitment. The issue of racial justice was "a moral issue . . . as old as the Scriptures and . . . as clear as the American Constitution," he said, and the time for delay had run out. His speech positioned the federal government as an active agency for southern change.

Of course, John F. Kennedy did not live to sign his bill into law. That honor fell to his successor, Lyndon B. Johnson, himself a Southerner, but also a legatee of New Deal reformism. Some southern legislators hoped he would allow them to weaken Kennedy's bill, but they were sadly mistaken. Wrapping himself in the mantle of the slain president, and shrewdly using his legislative skills as well as his acknowledged powers of persuasion, Johnson ensured that the bill passed substantially unchanged, and in so doing broke the political power of the white South. He signed the bill into law on July 2, 1964; it was "the great liberal achievement of the decade."[31]

During the long period between the introduction of the bill and the passage of the Civil Rights Act of 1964, Martin King's symbolic crowning as the most important African American of the twentieth century occurred. On August 28, 1963, two hundred fifty thousand Americans, black and white, joined him in a march on Washington in support of Kennedy's bill and for jobs and economic justice. It was a great day, still remembered for its nonviolence, for the spirit of idealism that motivated the marchers, but most of all for King's magnificent speech, with the Lincoln Memorial as backdrop. As he spoke of his dream, of a nation united in racial justice, where "one day on the red hills of Georgia the sons of former slaves and the sons of former slaveholders will be able to sit down together at the table of brotherhood," as he invoked the words of the old Negro spiritual, "Free at last! Free at last! Thank God almighty, we are free at last," he not only personified the spirit of the movement he had led so well, he provided the United States with one of the nobler moments of its history.

The federal government and the Civil Rights Movement did not, however, always work in such harmony. Indeed from the time SNCC volunteers first moved into the rural South in 1962, mainly to conduct the voter education projects they thought the Kennedys approved of, they complained that they were getting no protection from the FBI, the most visible government agency in the region. Instead, they and the community leaders they worked with were left at the mercy of their opponents, of which the Klan was only the most violent. SNCC workers were routinely shot at, arrested, and beaten, as were their local supporters, and some paid with their lives. Yet they persisted, the young activists constantly inspired by the courage of those they worked with, women like Mrs. Fanny Lou Hamer, of Ruleville, Mississippi. Mrs. Hamer, a semiliterate sharecropper when the SNCC volunteers came to town, was herself inspired by them into becoming one of the state's leading civil rights activists. In 1963 she was so severely beaten by local police that she never completely recovered. For SNCC workers, daily exposed to danger as they were, Martin King's exhortations "to love those who despitefully use you" in time rang hollow, as did the frequent claims by federal officials that the government was on the activists' side. They knew better. After all they had seen FBI men stand aside as local police attacked peaceful demonstrators with impunity. They had even seen their fellow workers murdered, without federal response.

Mrs. Hamer, soon to become a national figure as a result of her speech at the Democratic National Convention in 1964, was one of a long line of women activists whose participation was crucial to the movement's success. Like the textile strikers of the 1930s, black women fought for their freedom alongside men. Rosa Parks, after all, started it all off in Montgomery. Jo Ann Robinson, of Montgomery's Women's Political Council, channeled the community's outrage at Parks's arrest towards the idea of a boycott. In Little Rock, Daisy Bates sustained the nine black students throughout their long ordeal. In Nashville, Diane Nash not only led the movement that resulted in the desegregation of the downtown business area but played a crucial role the following year in ensuring that the freedom rides continued, despite the ferocity of the local white reaction and the indifference of the federal government. Ella Baker provided constant advice and support to the young SNCC activists as they thought through their philosophy and strategies. In Albany and in Birmingham, in Americus, Georgia, in Cambridge, Maryland, as well as Ruleville,

Mississippi, hundreds of brave local women both supported the volunteers who came to help them and joined actively in the struggle. They, too, walked the picket lines, they sat at the lunch counters, they ignored the insults, they took the blows.

It was out of the SNCC's anger, its sad conviction that only white deaths would prompt federal intervention, that the "Freedom Summer" was born in 1964. The brainchild of Robert Moses, its purpose was to flood the state of Mississippi with the affluent children of America's white middle class, briefly trained to do voter education work and to teach educationally deprived youngsters in "freedom schools." White America would sit up and take notice if they were harmed in any way, Moses and his fellow SNCC leaders reasoned. Their deaths, if any occurred, would surely not be ignored.

Such speculation all too soon became fact. The "Freedom Summer" had scarcely begun when three workers, Michael Schwerner, who had been running a voter education project in Meridian, Mississippi, since January, Andrew Goodman, a twenty-one-year-old Summer Project volunteer from New York, and James Chaney, a black Mississippian who had begun working for CORE, were reported missing in Neshoba County. They had been arrested there for speeding, held till after dark and then released, never to be seen alive again. They were, in fact, murdered by Klansmen and buried in an earthen dam.

Exactly as Moses had predicted, their disappearance sparked off a massive search by the FBI, assisted by hundreds of regular sailors, ordered there by President Johnson. But their bodies were not discovered for six weeks, and were only found then because a Klan informant led FBI agents to the site. By this time, national attention was elsewhere; not even the murder of white civil rights workers caused the nation to focus on Mississippi's violent society for more than a few days. The "Freedom Summer" continued, but against a backdrop of racist terror, of increasing tension between white and black workers, of growing disillusion with the federal government, and even of disillusion with Dr. King's nonviolent philosophy. As CORE's David Dennis shouted at James

Chaney's funeral, "I've got vengeance in my heart tonight. . . . If you go back home and sit down and take what these white men in Mississippi are doing to us . . . then God damn your souls." Nonviolence was a thing of the past for many SNCC and CORE field workers.

By the end of the "Freedom Summer," Mississippi's local workers had been given further reason to distrust federal government expressions of support and to doubt the sincerity of President Johnson's commitment. Robert Moses was the energizer of the idea of creating a new political party in Mississippi, the Mississippi Freedom Democratic Party, which would challenge the official Democratic delegation at the party's national convention in late August, on the grounds that blacks had heretofore been systematically excluded from state politics. Moses worked tirelessly to translate his idea into fact. So successful was he that by early August the MFDP had signed up sixty thousand members, who had elected a slate of sixty-eight delegates, including four whites, to attend the Democratic National Convention in Atlantic City. What happened there would determine the future relationship between the federal government and large sections of the Civil Rights Movement.

The MFDP delegates traveled to the convention brimming with confidence. They expected a fair hearing from the party's credentials committee, which they largely achieved, and a degree of media coverage, which was ensured when Fanny Lou Hamer described the brutality of everyday life in Mississippi. But they also expected President Johnson to support their challenge, and here they were mistaken. The president was furious at the attention they were getting and fearful that he would lose the support of other southern delegates as a result. He directed vice-presidential contender Hubert Humphrey to find a compromise. Humphrey turned the matter over to his protégé, Walter Mondale, who eventually came up with a solution that pleased no one except the president. The official Mississippi delegates would be seated provided they pledged to support the national ticket, but so would two members of the MFDP, as delegates at large. Moreover, the party pledged never again to accept delegates from states that disfranchised blacks. Though few were enthusiastic about the compromise, most activists, including Martin Luther King, urged the MFDP to accept it, on the grounds that it was crucial to maintain good relations with the White House. The respect some SNCC workers still had for King evaporated at that moment.

The MFDP delegates, new as they were to national politics, were in no mood to play political games. They "didn't come all this way for no two votes," declared Mrs. Hamer, as they left to go home to Mississippi rather than sit down with the enemy. Their friends had betrayed them, they angrily believed; they had proved beyond doubt the justice of their cause, but to what avail? The white liberals had hung them out to dry, and even Dr. King had deserted them. They were on their own; if they were to win their freedom, it would be through their own efforts alone.

They were, of course, wrong. It was Martin King who best understood the workings of American politics, and the fact that black civil rights could only be won through federal legislation, as the events of 1965 were to prove. This was when the last great battle of the civil rights years was fought; the terrain was Selma, Alabama, and the issue was the right to vote. Once again, King would combine the ingredients that had brought victory in Birmingham—a racist, baton-wielding sheriff, a specific issue, strong local community support, a well-planned mass action campaign, continued media attention, and a growing national consensus for change—to achieve further federal action. It was his most significant southern campaign.

Though the 1964 Civil Rights Act included provisions supposedly facilitating the right of southern blacks to register to vote, an analysis of the 1964 election showed that these provisions had not worked in the Deep South. Only 6 percent of Mississippi's voting age blacks had been registered, for example, 19 percent of Alabama's, 32 percent of Louisiana's, all states, incidentally, which Johnson's Republican opponent, Senator Barry Goldwater, had swept. There were political reasons, therefore, why the triumphant president, with huge liberal majorities in both houses, might be inclined to support further civil rights legislation specifically aimed at the right to vote. Martin King decided to find out whether the president would act.

King and his aides chose Selma after careful scrutiny. Situated in Dallas County, Alabama, it had a black population of fifteen thousand of whom only four hundred were registered to vote. It had an active black middle class to work with, and, equally important, an intransigent white minority, personified by the sheriff of Dallas County, the swaggering, violently racist Jim Clark. King was delighted with Clark. He was sure that once the SCLC came to town, the sheriff would lose control on national television, providing King with the footage he depended on.

And so it proved. Demonstrations and marches began in January, specifically directed at the issue of voting rights. "We are not asking for the ballot," said King at the opening of the campaign. "We are demanding it." In the succeeding weeks, Clark reacted as expected. He punched an SCLC leader in an incident that was shown on prime time television, and he arrested hundreds of marchers—usually with unnecessary force—including small children, as in Birmingham, and including Martin Luther King. By mid-February, national attention was directed at the events in Selma, and the president had already told King of his intention to send a voting rights message to Congress. The campaign could not have worked better.

In an attempt to increase the pressure, King announced on March 3 his plan to lead a march from Selma to the state capital, Montgomery, fifty-four miles away. This brought Alabama's Governor, George Wallace, into the action. He immediately banned the march, but the SCLC leaders decided to press on anyway. On March 7, therefore, six hundred marchers led by King's aide Hosea Williams and SCLC chairman John Lewis set out for Montgomery.

To reach U.S. Highway 80, the road to Montgomery, the marchers had to cross the Edmund Pettus Bridge on the outskirts of Selma. Scores of journalists had gathered there to record their progress, but so had Sheriff Clark's men, augmented by state troopers under the control of Major John Cloud. Without much warning the marchers were set upon and attacked with tear gas, cattle prods, chains, and batons as they tried to escape the violent men on horseback. It was the most savage assault on demonstrators in the whole civil rights period—and the most extensively filmed. Americans watched it on the network news that night and reacted as King hoped they would, with horror and with demands for voting rights legislation. Hundreds of people converged on Selma in solidarity with King and his fellow demonstrators. Clark and George Wallace between them had given voting rights a huge boost.

King, though shocked by the scale of the violence, decided to lead a second march on March 9 and asked for volunteers from all over the country to join him. However, Federal District Judge Frank Johnson banned the march temporarily, pending a hearing on its legality. In his whole career, King had never defied a federal court order. Would he do so now? The pressure on him was intense. SNCC militants, on the one hand, urged him to defy the ban; the president, on the other, urged him to hold off. In the end, he decided to compromise. Without telling his plans to those who followed him, he led fifteen hundred marchers on to the bridge but stopped when challenged and, after a brief prayer, led them back the way they had come. That was the end of King, as far as many SNCC members were concerned. They had joined the march only after the violence of March 7. Now they loudly proclaimed him to be a posturer, a man lacking in principle, a collaborator with the white power structure.

Once again they were wrong, for, even as the civil rights coalition was tearing itself apart, King and the philosophy he had come to exemplify enjoyed their greatest triumph. President Johnson was true to his word. As King waited in Selma, the president's aides rushed to complete a voting rights bill, and on March 15 Johnson spoke to a joint session of Congress about the issue— and to the nation, on all the networks. It was the most moving speech of his presidency. "Should we defeat every enemy," he said, even "should we double our wealth and conquer the stars,"

Americans would still "have failed as a people and a nation," if black citizens remained shut out of the national consensus. His bill would go a long way towards changing this situation. It would make it impossible for local voting registrars ever again "to flout the constitution." He spoke of the courage of America's black citizens in fighting peacefully for their rights and urged all his countrymen to make the cause their own. "All of us," he concluded, "must overcome the crippling legacy of bigotry and injustice. And we shall overcome." As the president repeated the refrain of the anthem of the Civil Rights Movement, tears ran down Martin Luther King's cheeks. He had won.

Only the march to Montgomery remained. Judge Johnson eventually permitted it to go ahead, and when Wallace still refused to protect the marchers, President Johnson federalized the Alabama National Guard and told them to do the job. King led his column over the Pettus Bridge on March 21, and four days later he spoke triumphantly to them from the steps of the state capitol in Montgomery, where the Civil Rights Movement, the most persistent and successful of southern activist movements, had begun ten years before. The uneasy coalition that had sustained it might have broken up, but this last victory belonged to all its components.

The voting rights bill swept through Congress, specifically targeting the various practices southern registrars had long used to keep blacks from the polls. In particular, it took aim at the literacy tests that local registrars had applied unfairly for decades, providing for their suspension in districts showing persistent patterns of discrimination and allowing federal registrars to place people directly on the rolls. Its effect was immediate. By 1968, 53 percent of eligible blacks were registered in Alabama, 60 percent in Louisiana, and, most dramatic of all, 44 percent in Mississippi, up from 6 percent in 1964. In Selma, where it had begun, the number had increased from 320 to 6,289, and Sheriff Clark was already out of office. Others of his ilk quickly followed, as blacks exercised their new ability to challenge their worst oppressors. King was surely correct in identifying the right to vote as the most important to be won, and federal legislation as the only permanent way of achieving it. The Civil Rights Movement had ended, but its legacy was a transformed South. In that sense, it remains easily the most important American social movement of the twentieth century.

Two southern governors, Jimmy Carter of Georgia and William Clinton of Arkansas, have been elected president since the civil rights battle was won. African Americans sit in all state legislatures, with the highest percentage in Mississippi; Virginia has even elected a black governor, the only southern state yet to do so; and mayoralties are now accessible to African Americans. Atlanta, Birmingham, and Memphis can all attest to that, as can scores of smaller towns and hamlets throughout the region. Martin Luther King and the southern activism he helped inspire brought it all about.

So successful was civil rights activism in destroying the southern caste system that it takes an effort of will to recollect the targets of the earlier activist tradition, especially the targets of the labor activists. True, the ending of segregation was always one of their aims, and here they could, with justice, retrospectively claim a small part in the ultimate victory. The textile mills, for example, now hire black workers; indeed they often comprise the majority of the work force.

But the unions are not there. The southern work force remains in 1999 as it was in 1914, largely unorganized, and becoming more so by the year. The aims of that strain of southern activism, so important in the 1930s and '40s, remain unfulfilled.

What of class? With the end of segregation, and the affirmative action drives that followed, some black Southerners have been able to join the economic elite and many more have become solidly middle class; the reformers of the SCHW would surely have welcomed this. But about 20 percent of the population of the old Confederacy still lies outside the circle of affluence. Black mayors now preside over cities divided into zones of wealth and poverty just as whites have historically done. Large parts of the rural South remain part of the nation's "number one economic problem," just as in 1938, and this the SCHW activists would surely find dispiriting, were they able to return. Moreover, racism remains, encoded in oblique language, vehemently denied publicly, but it remains nonetheless. Incidents such as the sickeningly brutal slaying of James Byrd in Jasper, Texas, in June 1998, dragged to his death by three white men while tied to their truck, remind us forcefully of that. In the year 2000, southern activism, dedicated to achieving a truly democratic, racially integrated region, and enormously successful in many ways, still has much work to do.

NOTES

1. W. J. Cash, *The Mind of the South* (New York: Knopf, 1941), 200; Jacquelyn Dowd Hall, Robert Korstad, and James LeLoudis, "Cotton Mill People: Work, Community and Progress in the Textile South, 1880–1940," *American Historical Review* 91, no. 2 (April 1986): 245.

2. These were the two constitutional amendments, passed during the Reconstruction era, that supposedly guaranteed *all* American citizens, including the recently freed slaves, equal rights under the law. The Fifteenth Amendment expressly dealt with the right to vote.

3. Cash, *Mind*, 245, 252.

4. George Tindall, *The Emergence of the New South, 1913–1945* (Baton Rouge: Louisiana University Press, 1967), 151–54.

5. Tindall, *Emergence*, 339.

6. Tindall, *Emergence*, 341.

7. John A. Salmond, *Gastonia 1929: The Story of the Loray Mill Strike* (Chapel Hill: University of North Carolina Press, 1995), 9.

8. Tindall, *Emergence*, 349.

9. Bryant Simon, "Prelude to the New Deal: The Political Response of South Carolina Textile Workers to the Great Depression," in *Race, Class and Community in Southern Labor History*, ed. Gary M. Fink and Merl E. Reed (Tuscaloosa: University of Alabama Press, 1994), 4.

10. Robert Zieger, *The CIO, 1935–1955* (Chapel Hill: University of North Carolina Press, 1995), 77.

11. Mary E. Frederickson, "A Place to Speak Our Minds," in *Working Lives: The Southern Exposure History of the South,* ed. Marc S. Miller (New York: Pantheon Books, 1980), 155.

12. John Egerton, *Speak Now against the Day* (New York: Knopf, 1994), 159.

13. Patricia Sullivan, *Days of Hope: Race and Democracy in the New Deal Era* (Chapel Hill: University of North Carolina Press, 1996), 151.

14. Egerton, *Speak Now*, 158.

15. Sullivan, *Days of Hope*, 73.

16. Robert F. Martin, "Critique of Southern Society and Vision of a New Order: The Fellowship of Southern Churches, 1934–1957," *Church History* 52 (March 1983): 66.

17. Sullivan, *Days of Hope*, 85.

18. Martha Gellhorn to Harry Hopkins, November 14, 1934. Harry Hopkins Papers, Franklin Delano Roosevelt Library, Hyde Park, New York.

19. Sullivan, *Days of Hope*, 99.

20. Egerton, *Speak Now*, 201.

21. Sullivan, *Race and Democracy*, 201.

22. Sullivan, *Race and Democracy*, 164.

23. Sullivan, *Race and Democracy*, 141–43.

24. The "four freedoms," which Franklin Roosevelt considered should be the birthright of everyone, and which had been incorporated into the Atlantic Charter, were freedom of speech and expression, freedom of worship, freedom from want, and freedom from fear.

25. Timothy Minchin, *What Do We Need a Union For? The TWUA in the South, 1945–1955* (Chapel Hill: University of North Carolina Press, 1997), 27.

26. Barbara Griffith, *The Crisis of American Labor: Operation Dixie and the Defeat of the CIO* (Philadelphia: Temple University Press, 1988), 60.

27. Numan V. Bartley, *The New South, 1945–1980* (Baton Rouge: Louisiana State University Press, 1995), 207.

28. Bartley, *New South*, 53.

29. John A. Salmond, *"My Mind Set on Freedom": A History of the Civil Rights Movement, 1954–1968* (Chicago: Ivan R. Dee, 1997), 64.

30. The White Citizens Council movement's aim was, through economic pressure, to deter African Americans from pushing for civil rights. The movement was particularly strong in the small towns of the Deep South.

31. Allen J. Matusow, *The Unraveling of America: A History of Liberalism in the 1960s* (New York: Harper, 1984), 95.

Documents

1

REPORT FROM MARTHA GELLHORN TO HARRY L. HOPKINS, DIRECTOR OF THE FEDERAL EMERGENCY RELIEF AGENCY, ON ECONOMIC CONDITIONS IN SOUTH CAROLINA FOLLOWING THE 1934 TEXTILE STRIKE (NOVEMBER 5, 1934)

Gellhorn, Martha
South Carolina
November 5, 1934

Report to Mr. Hopkins

My dear Mr. Hopkins:

My original report on South Carolina covers 62 pages; it is a bare and not very sprightly statement of facts; record of interviews; descriptions of homes, mill, people. This will have to be a tablet-form version. What generalizations I make are based on these records. I visited Columbia, Newberry, Whitmire, Greenwood, Anderson, Greenville, Spartanburg, and Rock Hill. Everywhere, I have attempted to interview the county administrator, and head Social Worker; Mill owners, Union Presidents, individual social workers, a doctor caring for textile workers, a doctor in charge of the county clinic, relief clients, textile workers; as many of these as possible in their native haunt. Sometimes this list is not complete and sometimes I have added a prominent business man, a mayor, a teacher, a judge. Within the limits of time (it's all pretty breathless) I have tried to get a check on every point of view noted, by listening to the opposition.

To begin with: the relief load is going up everywhere. This is due in part to oncoming winter; and also (in my area) to the fact that some mills have not reopened since the September strike, and that others have permanently discharged people involved in the strike. The general criticism of relief here is that it is a "dole" and is "pauperizing" people: by which the local gentry mean that relief clients refuse jobs in private industry. The main factual attack is against the 30¢ hourly work relief pay: local private pay for manual labor is between 7 1/2¢ to 10¢ an hour. This high government pay is just bananas to the low class manual labor (principally negro), which can now earn in two days what formerly took a week to earn. The criticism of the gov't rate of pay is echoed and underlined by everyone in the relief administration. They (county administrators, social workers) feel that this high pay is making relief too attractive, and swelling the rolls beyond reasonable limits. They advocate less pay and longer hours; so that the total relief would be the same (or preferably more) but that the relief clients would be occupied all week instead of a small fraction of a week. Another reason for the criticism of "giving money to people who don't need it," is that the local social workers are overloaded (sometimes carrying as high as 300 families, never less than 150); that they are not trained workers (simply because there is neither time nor funds to train them) and that therefore they can't properly check over and reduce the relief load. (There is the factual example of Oconeo County which was exclusively manned by local talent; the relief load mounted out of all proportion; the District Supervisor put in a trained worker and the load was cut two-thirds.) To finish up this relief question: I get a lot of anguish from local relief workers about the extent to which the general public "misunderstand" the aims and accomplishments of E.R.A. I know this is true from the comments I hear (business men; mill owners, etc.) And I do believe that there is a job of educational publicity to be done here, which would insure better cooperation with the local powers-that-be.

As for the relief itself, everywhere the authorities tell me that it is below subsistence level. This answers your questions about what relief is buying for the unemployed. Clothing is short everywhere; and this lack is one of the main sources of distress amongst both employed mill workers (who earn about the equivalent of work relief), and the unemployed. The relief organization attempts to give some household equipment when it is absolutely necessary. This below subsistence relief is probably not responsible for, but it is continuing, a chronic health condition. There is much pellagra here; (I have seen it ranging from a diseased skin condition to insanity).

There is anemia (as well as rickets, worms, bronchitis and other maladies due to lowered resistance) and all the doctors speak feelingly about the future of the children, from the health point of view. It would be unjust to base this dietary deficiency on relief; these people need education as much as they need food. Even when there is some money in a family (mill workers) the diet continues to be a menace of dried beans, cornbread, sorghum and meat. I should say that if one was fair one would say it is 50% poverty (food prices mounting as much as 200%) and 50% ignorance; in any case the race isn't going to be a hummer if this keeps up.

The relief clients here must be divided into three groups: first, negroes and border-line whites; second: industrial workers and tenant farmers; third: white collar. The first group is simply delighted with relief. Their attitude is that they're in on a good thing and are going to enjoy it while they can. Probably many of them are getting more for less effort than they ever have. The second class (all classes are needy; I'm merely discussing their outlook as far as I can determine it from visits, interviews, and talk with the responsible authorities), is that "the government is handing out something; I deserve it; and I'm going to get my share or complain." This is not universal; but it is average as an attitude. The white collar class is the hardest to study; if they are on work relief, they become broken and demoralised. Their pride is destroyed by the beggar-aspect of presenting charity orders. If they are absorbed into clerical projects, there is a marked tendency for the morale to improve. And I have seen cases, and had them cited, where a nervous condition (produced by despair) which bordered on insanity was corrected practically overnight by giving the man or woman, a job with some dignity and responsibility attached to it.

This is the attitude towards relief; but their attitude towards their own problems and the future is something else again. You suggested this question: "Is the sense of insecurity spreading." I should say that "spreading" was an erroneous word. It's here. In every shape and form; in every class. Take the low-class relief cases; their fear is that the government will stop feeding them, that the winter will be cold and no one will give them shoes and coats, coal or shelter. The industrial worker, employed, lives in a kind of feverish terror about his job. (I think this terror is largely responsible for labor disturbances here.) He is frightened that the mill will close; or run at such reduced time that his wage will not suffice for food. (They can't buy more than food anyhow.) He is frightened that he can't maintain the required speed of production, will fall behind in his work and be dropped. He is frightened that his boss will find an excuse to drop him if he's a Union man (and you see the most extraordinary secrecy and fear and dishonesty, relating to this Union question, on both sides of the capitalist fence.) He is frightened of the winter; of having no clothes; of being unable to send his children to school. The white collar worker is in the same boat, though probably with less specialized or immediately material fears. It goes from the bottom to the top; mill owners show me ledgers which are beautifully done in red ink; they all tell me (with one exception) that business is worse than last year; there is a lack of confidence, no demand, etc. etc. I have a feeling that people are good and panicked. This is cheerful news to send on.

As a footnote to this sense of insecurity; no employer has said that he would increase employment within the next 3 to 6 months. On the contrary, they have all said they expect to curtail; though they do not mean to put men out of work, they expect to put them on part time work. Naturally this gets around; and doesn't increase the worker's calm and peace of mind. Likewise rumors are rife (and have been fostered in the press in a vague, whispering way) that the Federal Government is going to close up relief here in January. All this soothes no one.

But despite this sense of insecurity, I am astonished by the good humor, or faith or apathy (or even good sense) of the unemployed; and the still (but not very happily) employed. There are no protest groups. There are no "dangerous reds." If anything, these people are a sad grey; waiting, hoping, trusting. They talk of the President very much as if he were Moses, and they are simply waiting to be led into the promised land. Sometimes textile workers talk of Gorman's promises. Anyhow they are all banking on someone (if it's only the "Supreme Being," as one UTW president told me.) There is no revolutionary talk; and the mere suggestion of violence is rejected. The strikers are all proud of being "peace-loving" men and tell you with joy that "there wasn't even a fist-fight" and never will be. I think the problem is not one of fighting off a "red menace" (those two goofy words made me mad every time I see them); but of fighting off hopelessness; despair; a dangerous feeling of helplessness and dependence. On the other hand, I think that if relief were suddenly stopped there might be some trouble; of the kind that consists in breaking in grocery store windows which used to occur at the end of the last regime. And I do think that if, in time, the industrial workers here don't feel that their grievances have been settled (*"feel"*), their disillusionment might take some active form. Probably another peaceful, abortive, useless strike. At the moment however "we're counting on the President; he's a man of his word and he won't let us down."

I can't too much emphasize my impression that the problem is not one of an oncoming revolution, for which the Legion and the D.A.R. had best prepare. I think a good many more deceptions and a great deal more suffering and hunger (years in short, and lean unrelieved years at that) must come, before this part of the world will take to guns and pitch-forks. But I think there is a terrible problem here of salvaging human material; or letting it permanently rot. And, as far as I can find, in talking with all the competent people, relief is not touching this problem. Present relief is a kind of hypodermic; it doesn't take long to realize that this ailment is chronic and needs long-time, constructive planning to re-train people and re-establish them (in some other role or capacity) in society.

The health problem is really terrific. Inadequate medical set-ups for the poor; and ignorance. Syphilis is, practically speaking, uncured and unchecked; and to use the words of a doctor who runs a county v. d. clinic, "it is spreading like wild fire." I don't mean that this condition is special to this period; but here it is. Another fine problem is that of birth control. In the relief rolls it is an accepted fact that the more incapable and unequipped (physically, mentally, materially) the parents, the more offspring they produce. Which offspring are in degeneration from their parents; and can merely swell the relief rolls, aiding neither themselves nor the community. I can't see where or why this thing should stop; unless—in conjunction with relief—there are clinics; both to care for and improve present health, and to check the increase of unwanted, unprovided for, and unequipped children.

This is perhaps too sketchy a report; if it is, my appalling 62 page opus can be sent along to bolster up with names, places, facts, everything herein stated. I'm full of ideas which can't possibly interest you; you sent us out to do a reporting job which I hope will be satisfactorily done. Have spent two days in North Carolina; and it seems at once better and worse than its neighboring state in various respects. But that report will come along at the end of the week.

MARTHA GELLHORN

Charlotte, North Carolina
November 5

2

THE UNANIMOUS OPINION OF THE SUPREME COURT IN *BROWN V. THE BOARD OF EDUCATION OF TOPEKA, KANSAS* (1954)

W arren, c.j., These cases come to us from the States of Kansas, South Carolina, Virginia, and Delaware. They are premised on different facts and different local conditions, but a common legal question justifies their consideration together in this consolidated opinion.

In each of the cases, minors of the Negro race, through their legal representatives, seek the aid of the courts in obtaining admission to the public schools of their community on a nonsegregated basis. In each instance, they had been denied admission to schools attended by white children under laws requiring or permitting segregation according to race. This segregation was alleged to deprive the plaintiffs of the equal protection of the laws under the Fourteenth Amendment. . . . The plaintiffs contend that segregated public schools are not "equal" and cannot be made "equal," and that hence they are deprived of the equal protection of the laws. Because of the obvious importance of the question presented, the Court took jurisdiction. Argument was heard in the 1952 Term, and reargument was heard this Term on certain questions propounded by the Court.

Reargument was largely devoted to the circumstances surrounding the adoption of the Fourteenth Amendment in 1868. It covered exhaustively consideration of the Amendment in Congress, ratification by the states, then existing practices in racial segregation, and the views of proponents and opponents of the Amendment. This discussion and our own investigation convince us that, although these sources cast some light, it is not enough to resolve the problem with which we are faced. At best, they are inconclusive. The most avid proponents of the post-War Amendments undoubtedly intended them to remove all legal distinctions among "all persons born or naturalized in the United States." Their opponents, just as certainly, were antagonistic to both the letter and the spirit of the Amendments and wished them to have the most limited effect. What others in Congress and the state legislatures had in mind cannot be determined with any degree of certainty.

An additional reason for the inconclusive nature of the Amendment's history, with respect to segregated schools, is the status of public education at that time. In the South, the movement toward free common schools, supported by general taxation, had not yet taken hold. Education of white children was largely in the hands of private groups. Education of Negroes was almost non-existent, and practically all of the race were illiterate. In fact, any education of Negroes was forbidden by law in some states. Today, in contrast, many Negroes have achieved outstanding success in the arts and sciences as well as in the business and professional world. It is true that public school education at the time of the Amendment had advanced further in the North, but the effect of the Amendment on Northern States was generally ignored in the congressional debates. Even in the North, the conditions of public education did not approximate those existing today. The curriculum was usually rudimentary; ungraded schools were common in rural areas; the school term was but three months a year in many states; and compulsory school attendance was virtually unknown. As a consequence, it is not surprising that there should be so little in the history of the Fourteenth Amendment relating to its intended effect on public education.

In the first cases in this Court construing the Fourteenth Amendment, decided shortly after its adoption, the Court interpreted it as proscribing all state-imposed discriminations against the Negro race. The doctrine of "separate but equal" did not make its appearance in this Court until 1896 in the case of *Plessy v. Ferguson,* involving not education but transportation. American courts have since labored with the doctrine for over half a century. . . .

The Negro and white schools involved [here] have been equalized, or are being equalized, with respect to buildings, curricula, qualifications and salaries of teachers, and other "tangible" factors. Our decision, therefore, cannot turn on merely a comparison of these tangible factors in the Negro and white schools involved in each of the cases. We must look instead to the effect of segregation itself on public education.

In approaching this problem, we cannot turn the clock back to 1868 when the Amendment was adopted, or even to 1896 when *Plessy v. Ferguson* was written. We must consider public education in the light of its full development and its present place in American life throughout the Nation. Only in this way can it be determined if segregation in public schools deprives these plaintiffs of the equal protection of the laws.

Today, education is perhaps the most important function of state and local governments. Compulsory school attendance laws and the great expenditures for education both demonstrate our recognition of the importance of education to our democratic society. It is required in the performance of our most basic public responsibilities, even service in the armed forces. It is the very foundation of good citizenship. Today it is a principal instrument in awakening the child to cultural values, in preparing him for later professional training, and in helping him to adjust normally to his environment. In these days it is doubtful that any child may reasonably be expected to succeed in life if he is denied the opportunity of an education. Such an opportunity, where the state has undertaken to provide it, is a right which must be made available to all on equal terms.

We come then to the question presented: Does segregation of children in public schools solely on the basis of race, even though the physical facilities and other "tangible" factors may be equal, deprive the children of the minority group of equal educational opportunities? We believe that it does. . . .

To separate them from others of similar age and qualifications solely because of their race generates a feeling of inferiority as to their status in the community that may affect their hearts and minds in a way unlikely ever to be undone. The effect of this separation on their educational opportunities was well stated by a finding in the Kansas case by a court which nevertheless felt compelled to rule against the Negro plaintiffs:

> "Segregation of white and colored children in public schools has a detrimental effect upon the colored children. The impact is greater when it has the sanction of the law; for the policy of separating the races is usually interpreted as denoting the inferiority of the negro group. A sense of inferiority affects the motivation of a child to learn. Segregation with the sanction of law, therefore has a tendency to [retard] the educational and mental development of negro children and to deprive them of some of the benefits they would receive in a racial[ly] integrated school system."

Whatever may have been the extent of psychological knowledge at the time of *Plessy v. Ferguson,* this finding is amply supported by modern authority. Any language in *Plessy v. Ferguson* contrary to this finding is rejected. We conclude that in the field of public education the doctrine of "separate but equal" has no place. Separate educational facilities are inherently unequal. Therefore, we hold that the plaintiffs and others similarly situated for whom the actions have been brought are, by reason of the segregation complained of, deprived of the equal protection of the laws guaranteed by the Fourteenth Amendment. . . .

Because these are class actions, because of the wide applicability of this decision, and because of the great variety of local conditions, the formulation of decrees in these cases presents problems of considerable complexity. On reargument, the consideration of appropriate relief was necessarily subordinated to the primary question—the constitutionality of segregation in public education. We have now announced that such segregation is a denial of the equal protection of the laws. In order that we may have the full assistance of the parties in formulating decrees, the cases will be restored to the docket, and the parties are requested to present further argument on Questions 4 and 5 [dealing with the implementation of the decision] previously propounded by the Court for the reargument of this Term.

3

THE DECLARATION OF NINETY-SIX SOUTHERN CONGRESSMEN AGAINST THE *BROWN* DECISION (MARCH 12, 1956)

W e regard the decision of the Supreme Court in the school cases as clear abuse of judicial power. It climaxes a trend in the Federal judiciary undertaking to legislate, in derogation of the authority of Congress, and to encroach upon the reserved rights of the states and the people.

The original Constitution does not mention education. Neither does the Fourteenth Amendment nor any other amendment. The debates preceding the submission of the Fourteenth Amendment clearly show that there was no intent that it should affect the systems of education maintained by the states.

The very Congress which proposed the amendment subsequently provided for segregated schools in the District of Columbia.

When the amendment was adopted in 1868, there were thirty-seven states of the Union. Every one of the twenty-six states that had any substantial racial differences among its people either approved the operation of segregated schools already in existence or subsequently established such schools by action of the same law-making body which considered the Fourteenth Amendment.

As admitted by the Supreme Court in the public school case (*Brown v. Board of Education*), the Doctrine of separate but equal

174

schools "apparently originated in *Roberts v. City of Boston* (1849), upholding school segregation against attack as being violative of a state constitutional guarantee of equality." This constitutional doctrine began in the North—not in the South—and it was followed not only in Massachusetts but in Connecticut, New York, Illinois, Indiana, Michigan, Minnesota, New Jersey, Ohio, Pennsylvania and other northern states until they, exercising their rights as states through the constitutional processes of local self-government, changed their school systems.

In the case of *Plessy v. Ferguson* in 1896 the Supreme Court expressly declared that under the Fourteenth Amendment no person was denied any of his rights if the states provided separate but equal public facilities. This decision has been followed in many other cases. It is notable that the Supreme Court, speaking through Chief Justice Taft, a former President of the United States, unanimously declared in 1927 in *Lum v. Rice* that the "separate but equal" principle is ". . . within the discretion of the state in regulating its public schools and does not conflict with the Fourteenth Amendment."

This interpretation, restated time and again, became a part of the life of the people of many of the states and confirmed their habits, customs, traditions and way of life. It is founded on elemental humanity and common sense, for parents should not be deprived by Government of the right to direct the lives and education of their own children.

Though there has been no constitutional amendment or act of Congress changing this established legal principle almost a century old, the Supreme Court of the United States, with no legal basis for such action, undertook to exercise their naked judicial power and substituted their personal political and social ideas for the established law of the land.

This unwarranted exercise of power by the court, contrary to the Constitution, is creating chaos and confusion in the states principally affected. It is destroying the amicable relations between the white and Negro races that have been created through ninety years of patient effort by the good people of both races. It has planted hatred and suspicion where there has been heretofore friendship and understanding.

Without regard to the consent of the governed, outside agitators are threatening immediate and revolutionary changes in our public school systems. If done, this is certain to destroy the system of public education in some of the states.

With the gravest concern for the explosive and dangerous condition created by this decision and inflamed by outside meddlers:

We reaffirm our reliance on the Constitution as the fundamental law of the land.

We decry the Supreme Court's encroachments on rights reserved to the states and to the people, contrary to established law and to the Constitution.

We commend the motives of those states which have declared the intention to resist forced integration by any lawful means.

We appeal to the states and people who are not directly affected by these decisions to consider the constitutional principles involved against the time when they too, on issues vital to them, may be the victims of judicial encroachment.

Even though we constitute a minority in the present Congress, we have full faith that a majority of the American people believe in the dual system of government which has enabled us to achieve our greatness and will in time demand that the reserved rights of the states and of the people be made secure against judicial usurpation.

We pledge ourselves to use all lawful means to bring about a reversal of this decision which is contrary to the Constitution and to prevent the use of force in its implementation.

In this trying period, as we all seek to right this wrong, we appeal to our people not to be provoked by the agitators and troublemakers invading our states and to scrupulously refrain from disorder and lawless acts.

4

MARTIN LUTHER KING'S "I HAVE A DREAM" SPEECH, GIVEN AT THE CONCLUSION OF THE MARCH ON WASHINGTON (AUGUST 28, 1963)

Five score years ago, a great American, in whose symbolic shadow we stand, signed the Emancipation Proclamation. This momentous decree came as a great beacon light of hope to millions of Negro slaves who have been seared in the flames of withering injustice. It came as a joyous daybreak to end the long night of captivity.

But one hundred years later, we must face the tragic fact that the Negro is still not free. One hundred years later, the life of the Negro is still sadly crippled by the manacles of segregation and the chains of discrimination. One hundred years later, the Negro lives on a lonely island of poverty in the midst of a vast ocean of material prosperity. One hundred years later, the Negro is still languished in the corners of American society and finds himself an exile in his own land. So we have come here today to dramatize an appalling condition.

In a sense we have come to our nation's Capitol to cash a check. When the architects of our republic wrote the magnificent words of the Constitution and the Declaration of Independence, they were signing a promissory note to which every American was to fall heir. This note was a promise that all men would be guaranteed the unalienable rights of life, liberty, and the pursuit of happiness.

It is obvious today that America has defaulted on this promissory note insofar as her citizens of color are concerned. Instead of honoring this sacred obligation, America has given the Negro people a bad check; a check which has come back marked "insufficient funds." But we refuse to believe that the bank of justice is bankrupt. We refuse to believe that there are insufficient funds in the great vaults of opportunity of this nation. So we have come to cash this check—a check that will give us upon demand the riches of freedom and the security of justice. . . .

It would be fatal for the nation to overlook the urgency of the moment and to underestimate the determination of the Negro. This sweltering summer of the Negro's legitimate discontent will not pass until there is an invigorating autumn of freedom and equality. 1963 is not an end, but a beginning. Those who hope that the Negro needed to blow off steam and will now be content will have a rude awakening if the Nation returns to business as usual. There will be neither rest nor tranquility in America until the Negro is granted his citizenship rights. The whirlwinds of revolt will continue to shake the foundations of our Nation until the bright day of justice emerges.

But there is something that I must say to my people.

. . . In the process of gaining our rightful place we must not be guilty of wrongful deeds. Let us not seek to satisfy our thirst for freedom by drinking from the cup of bitterness and hatred.

We must forever conduct our struggle on the high plane of dignity and discipline. We must not allow our creative protest to degenerate into physical violence. Again and again we must rise to the majestic heights of meeting physical force with soul force. The marvelous new militancy which has engulfed the Negro community must not lead us to a distrust of all white people, for many of our white brothers, as evidenced by their presence here today, have come to realize that their destiny is tied up with our destiny and their freedom is inextricably bound to our freedom. We cannot walk alone.

And as we walk, we must make the pledge that we shall march ahead. We cannot turn back. There are those who are asking the devotees of civil rights, "when will you be satisfied?" We can never be satisfied as long as the Negro is the victim of the unspeakable horrors of police brutality. We can never be satisfied as long as our bodies, heavy with the fatigue of travel, cannot gain lodging in the motels of the highways and the hotels of the cities. We cannot be satisfied as long as the Negro's basic mobility is from a smaller ghetto to a larger one. We can never be satisfied as long as a Negro in Mississippi cannot vote and a Negro in New York believes he has nothing for which to vote. No, no we are not satisfied, and we will not be satisfied until justice rolls down like waters and righteousness like a mighty stream.

I am not unmindful that some of you have come here out of great trials and tribulations. Some of you have come fresh from narrow jail cells. Some of you have come from areas where your quest for freedom left you battered by the storms of persecution and staggered by the winds of police brutality. You have been the veterans of creative suffering. Continue to work with the faith that unearned suffering is redemptive.

Go back to Mississippi, go back to Alabama, go back to South Carolina, go back to Georgia, go back to Louisiana, go back to the slums and ghettos of our northern cities, knowing that somehow this situation can and will be changed. Let us not wallow in the valley of despair.

I say to you today, my friends, that in spite of the difficulties and frustrations of the moment I still have a dream. It is a dream deeply rooted in the American dream.

I have a dream that one day this nation will rise up and live out the true meaning of its creed: "We hold these truths to be self-evident; that all men are created equal."

I have a dream that one day even the state of Mississippi, a desert state sweltering with the heat of injustice and oppression, will be transformed into an oasis of freedom and justice.

I have a dream that my four little children will one day live in a nation where they will not be judged by the color of their skin but by the content of their character.

I have a dream today.

I have a dream that one day the state of Alabama, whose governor's lips are presently dripping with the words of interposition and nullification, will be transformed into a situation where little black boys and black girls will be able to join hands with little white boys and white girls and walk together as sisters and brothers.

I have a dream today.

I have a dream that one day every valley shall be exalted, every hill and mountain shall be made low, the rough places will be made plains, and the crooked places will be made straight, and the glory of the Lord shall be revealed, and all flesh shall see it together.

This is our hope. This is the faith with which I return to the South. With this faith we will be able to hew out of the mountain of despair a stone of hope. With this faith we will be able to transform the jangling discords of our nation into a beautiful symphony of brotherhood. With this faith we will be able to work together, to pray together, to struggle together, to go to jail together, to stand up for freedom together, knowing that we will be free one day.

BIBLIOGRAPHY

Bartley, Numan V. *The New South 1945–1980: The Story of the South's Modernization*. Baton Rouge: Louisiana Sate University Press, 1995.

Branch, Taylor. *Parting the Waters: America in the King Years, 1954–1963*. New York: Simon and Schuster, 1988.

———. *Pillar of Fire: America in the King Years, 1963–65*. New York: Simon and Schuster, 1998.

Brooks, Cleanth. "William Faulkner." In *The History of Southern Literature*, ed. Louis D. Rubin, Jr., Blyden Jackson, Rayburn S. Moore, Lewis P. Simpson, and Thomas Daniel Young. Baton Rouge: Louisiana State University Press, 1985.

Cash, W. J. *The Mind of the South*. New York: Knopf, 1941.

Clayton, Bruce. *The Savage Ideal: Intolerance and Intellectual Leadership in the South, 1890–1914*. Baltimore: The Johns Hopkins University Press, 1972.

———. "Race, Gender, and Modernism: the Case of Lillian Smith." In *Varieties of Southern History: New Essays on a Region and Its People*, ed. Bruce Clayton and John A. Salmond. Westport, Conn.: Greenwood Press, 1996.

———. *W. J. Cash: A Life*. Baton Rouge: Louisiana State University Press, 1991.

Clayton, Bruce, and John A. Salmond, eds. *The South Is Another Land: Essays on the Twentieth Century South*. Wesport, Conn.: Greenwood Press, 1987.

Daniel, Pete. *Standing at the Crossroads: Southern Life in the Twentieth Century*. New York: Hill and Wang, 1986.

Dunbar, Anthony. *Against the Grain: Southern Radicals and Prophets, 1929–1959*. Charlottesville: University of Virginia Press, 1981.

Egerton, John. *Speak Now Against the Day: the Generation Before the Civil Rights Movement.* New York: Knopf, 1994.

Fairclough, Adam. *Martin Luther King, Jr.* Athens: University of Georgia Press, 1995.

Franklin, John Hope. *From Slavery to Freedom: A History of African Americans.* New York: McGraw-Hill, Inc., 1947, 1994.

Gatewood, Willard B., Jr., *Preachers, Pedagogues & Politicians: The Evolution Controversy in North Carolina, 1920–27.* Chapel Hill: University of North Carolina Press, 1966.

Goldfield, David. *Black, White and Southern: Race Relations and Southern Culture, 1940 to the Present.* Baton Rouge: Louisiana State University Press, 1990.

Goldfield, David R. *Promised Land: The South Since 1945.* Arlington Heights, Ill.: Harlan Davidson, Inc., 1987.

Grantham, Dewey W. *The South in Modern America: A Region at Odds.* New York: HarperCollins Publishers, Inc., 1994.

Griffith, Barbara. *The Crisis of American Labor. Operation Dixie and the Defeat of the CIO.* Philadelphia: Temple University Press, 1986.

Hall, Jaqueline Dowd, James LeLoudis, Robert Korstad, Mary Murphy, Lu Ann Jones, and Christopher B. Daly. *Like a Family: The Making of a Southern Cotton Mill World.* Chapel Hill: University of North Carolina Press, 1987.

Hobson, Fred. *Serpent in Eden: H. L. Mencken and the South.* Baton Rouge: Louisiana State University Press, 1974.

————. *Tell About the South: The Southern Rage to Explain.* Baton Rouge: Louisiana State University Press, 1983.

Jones, Anne Goodwyn. *Tomorrow Is Another Day: The Woman Writer in the South, 1859–1936.* Baton Rouge: Louisiana State University Press, 1981.

Kelley, Robin. *Hammer and Hoe: Alabama Communists During the Great Depression.* Chapel Hill: University of North Carolina Press, 1990.

King, Martin Luther, Jr. *Stride Toward Freedom: The Montgomery Story.* New York: Harper and Brothers, 1958.

————. *Why We Can't Wait.* New York: Mentor Books, 1963, 1964.

King, Richard H. *A Southern Renaissance: The Cultural Awakening of the American South, 1930–1955.* New York: Oxford University Press, 1980.

Kneebone, John T. *Southern Liberal Journalists and the Issue of Race, 1920–1944.* Chapel Hill: University of North Carolina Press, 1985.

Lewis, David L. *King: A Biography.* Urbana: University of Illinois Press, 1978.

Logan, Rayford. *The Negro in American Life and Thought: The Nadir, 1877–1901.* New York: Dial Press, 1954.

Marable, Manning. *Race, Reform and Rebellion; The Second Reconstruction in Black America 1945–1982.* Jackson: University Press of Mississippi, 1984.

Minchin, Timothy. *What Do We Need a Union For? The TWUA in the South, 1945–1955.* Chapel Hill: University of North Carolina Press, 1997.

O'Brien, Michael. *The Idea of the American South, 1920–1941.* Baltimore: The Johns Hopkins University Press, 1979.

Reed, Linda. *Simple Decency and Common Sense: the Southern Conference Movement, 1938–1963.* Bloomington: University of Indiana Press, 1991.

Salmond, John. *Gastonia 1929: The Story of the Loray Mill Strike.* Chapel Hill: University of North Carolina Press, 1995.

———. *Miss Lucy of the CIO: The Life and Times of Lucy Randolph Mason, 1882–1959.* Athens: University of Georgia Press, 1988.

———. *"My Mind Set on Freedom": A History of the Civil Rights Movement, 1954–1968.* Chicago: Ivan R. Dee, 1997.

———. *A Southern Rebel: The Life and Times of Aubrey Willis Williams.* Chapel Hill: University of North Carolina Press, 1983.

Singal, Daniel Joseph. *The War Within: From Victorian to Modernist Thought in the South, 1919–1945.* Chapel Hill: University of North Carolina Press, 1982.

Sitkoff, Harvard. *The Struggle for Black Equality, 1954–1980.* New York: Oxford University Press, 1981.

Sullivan, Patricia. *Days of Hope: Race and Democracy in the New Deal Era.* Chapel Hill: University of North Carolina Press, 1996.

Tindall, George B. *The Emergence of the New South, 1913–1945.* Baton Rouge: Louisiana State University Press, 1967.

Washington, James M., ed. *A Testament of Hope: The Essential Writings of Martin Luther King, Jr.* San Francisco: HarperSanFrancisco, 1986.

Williamson, Joel. *William Faulkner and Southern History.* New York: Oxford University Press, 1993.

Wilson, Charles Reagan, and William Ferris, eds. *Encyclopedia of Southern Culture.* Chapel Hill: University of North Carolina Press, 1989.

Woodward, C. Vann. *The Burden of Southern History.* Baton Rouge: Louisiana State University Press, 1960, 1968.

———. *The Strange Career of Jim Crow.* New York: Oxford University Press, 1955, 1974.

Wright, Richard. *Black Boy.* New York: Harper and Brothers, 1945.

ACKNOWLEDGMENTS

Documents following Bruce Clayton's essay, "Southern Intellectuals":

1. Excerpts from Gerald W. Johnson's "Saving Souls," *American Mercury* 2 (May–August 1924): 364–68.
2. Excerpt from "Ode to the Confederate Dead" from *The Collected Poems 1919–1976* by Allen Tate. Copyright © 1977 by Allen Tate. Reprinted by permission of Farrar, Straus & Giroux, LLC.
3. William Faulkner's Nobel Prize speech: available at http://www.mcsr.olemiss.edu/~egjbp/faulkner/nobel.html. Accessed 18 August 1998.
4. Excerpt from a letter from Lillian Smith to Martin Luther King, Jr., dated March 10, 1956: from *How Am I to Be Heard? Letters of Lillian Smith,* ed. Margaret Rose Gladney (Chapel Hill: University of North Carolina Press, 1993), 193–95.
5. Excerpt from Martin Luther King, Jr.'s letter from Birmingham City Jail from *A Testament of Hope: The Essential Writings of Martin Luther King, Jr.,* ed. James M. Washington (San Francisco: HarperSanFrancisco, 1986), 289–302.

Documents following John Salmond's essay, "The South in the Depression Decades":

1. Report from Martha Gellhorn to Harry L. Hopkins: from the papers of Harry L. Hopkins.
2. *Brown v. the Board of Education of Topeka, Kansas,* 347 U.S. 483.
3. Declaration of Ninety-Six Southern Congressmen: *Congressional Record,* 84th Congress, 2d Session, p. 4460.
4. Excerpts from Martin Luther King's "I Have a Dream Speech" from *The Civil Rights Reader,* ed. Leon Friedman (New York: Walker and Company, 1968), pp. 110–13.

INDEX

ABOUT THE AUTHORS

Bruce Clayton is the Harry A. Logan, Sr., Professor of History at Allegheny College in Meadville, Pennsylvania. He is the author of *The Savage Ideal: Intolerance and Intellectual Leadership in the South, 1890–1914* (1972); *W.J. Cash: A Life* (1991); *Praying for Base Hits: An American Boyhood* (1998); and co-editor with John Salmond of two books of essays on the South: *The South Is Another Land: Essays on the Twentieth-Century South* (1987) and *Varieties of Southern History: New Essays on a Region and Its People* (1996). Clayton holds a Ph.D. in history from Duke University and has been the recipient of numerous prizes and awards. He has reviewed widely for scholarly journals and newspapers including the *Atlanta Journal Constitution,* the *Baltimore Sun,* and the *Philadelphia Inquirer.* He was a Fulbright Senior Lecturer in New Zealand in 1995.

John Salmond is Professor of American History and Pro Vice Chancellor at La Trobe University, Melbourne, Australia. He is the author of numerous books and articles on aspects of American history, the most recent being *"My Mind Set on Freedom": A History of the Civil Rights Movement, 1954–1968* (1997); *Varieties of Southern History: New Essays on a Region and Its People* (1996) edited with Bruce Clayton; and *Gastonia 1929: The Story of the Loray Mill Strike* (1995).